LAW OF THE LAND

A Practical Legal Guide for Tourists and Business Travelers

Spain

By Michael L. Moore Esq.

DEDICATION

This book is dedicated to the memory of my late older brother, Kenneth Lee Moore, whose tragic murder at 15 years of age inspired me to write this series of books.

This book is also dedicated to my parents, John Henry Moore, and Edna Mae Moore, whose tremendous parenting skills kept me focused on the important things in life: being reverent, getting educated, and prioritizing family.

Finally, this book is dedicated to my beautiful family, my wife Royellen, my son AJ, and my daughter Karla. They inspire me every single day to be kind, patient, and compassionate.

IN LOVING MEMORY OF:

Belinda Joyce Moore Moss—my beautiful and wonderful sister, who supported me in every positive thing that I ever attempted to do.

Michael Eugene Baker—my dedicated and loyal friend and brother, who always wanted the very best for me.

Sylvia Joyce Hill—my eldest sister, who had a beautiful spirit and was like a second mother to me.

Travel smart. Stay legal. Stay safe.®

From local laws to medical guides we've got you covered world wide
in one digital platform.

PREFACE

My introduction to the justice system came when I was only 10 years old. My 15-year-old brother was murdered with a butcher knife by a 19-year-old in a simple argument over a torn shirt. I was devastated by his death and sought retribution for his fate that never came. The woman was initially charged with second degree murder, but after plea negotiations, she was convicted of manslaughter and sentenced to only five years in a youthful offender school and ordered to undergo psychiatric care. That was it. Nothing more. The judicial system had run its course.

My family knew nothing about the justice system, and we did not have the tools to advocate for ourselves. No one provided us with a written source to reference for guidance through this process. There was no easily accessible, easy to understand, definitive source to educate ourselves about the legal system that we suddenly and unexpectedly found ourselves immersed in after being victimized by such a violent criminal act.

As I got older, finished college, law school, and ultimately started practicing law, it became clear to me that most people are not knowledgeable about the law or how the judicial process works. If most people are uninformed here in the United States regarding the law and the legal process, how would they fare when in other countries? I realized that tourists and businesspeople who travel internationally needed access to information on how to navigate the legal system in other countries!

For many years, there has been considerable media attention focused on international travelers experiencing legal difficulties while traveling abroad. Most of these news stories gained attention in the United States and abroad because they involved American citizens facing punishment that was considered "unconventional" and "harsh" by United States' legal standards. I recall a news story in 1994 regarding Michael Fay, a young American male, who had broken the law in Singapore. He was convicted and sentenced to be caned and or whipped publicly. While the United States Government weighed in on the inappropriate and cruel nature of the punishment, the young American was beaten because he had been convicted under Singapore law.

Similarly, in recent years, international news stories have garnered headlines regarding foreign travelers and their issues with the laws of countries that were not their own. Amanda Knox, an American woman, was accused of murdering her roommate in Italy in 2007 and spent almost four years in an Italian prison before being definitively acquitted by the Supreme Court of Cassatio. Kenneth Bae, an American citizen, was arrested in North Korea in 2012 and was convicted for hostile acts against the communist country. He was sentenced to 15 years hard labor but was released in 2014 after efforts by the U.S. State Department. More recently, United States Basketball Star, Brittany Griner was arrested in February 2022 at a Moscow airport on drug-related charges and detained for nearly 10 months, spending much of that time in prison. Her plight unfolded at the same time Russia invaded Ukraine and further heightened tensions between Russia and the United States, ending only after she was freed in exchange for a notorious Russian arms dealer.

It was in 1994 that another personal tragic event occurred that finally inspired me to write these series of books. A dear friend and also client of mine was brutally murdered while on his second honeymoon in Jamaica. News of his murder shocked me and our local community. The legal hurdles his family had to overcome to see that justice was properly dispensed far away from home, in another country, with an entirely different set of criminal procedural rules and laws, was difficult to navigate.

As I was my friend's attorney at the time of his death, his family asked that I act as their "legal liaison" to the Jamaican Prosecutor's Office and to the Jamaican Police Department. I participated in multiple police interviews with my client's widow because she was the primary witness to his murder. As a former prosecuting attorney, I was also allowed by the Court, as a professional courtesy, to sit at the prosecutor's table to consult with the prosecuting attorney during trial. What I observed about the Jamaican trial process from a front row seat was compelling enough to cause me to seriously consider educating the "world" regarding what to expect and how to act appropriately when faced with legal issues while traveling abroad.

One of the realities in life is that, regardless of what country you are in, it is never a pleasant experience to run afoul of the law and be forced to accept that someone else will be making a decision about your pecuniary, proprietary, or penal interests (your money, your property, or your freedom).

It is important to know what the laws are, how they apply to you, and how to navigate the legal system if you are charged with a crime. It is also very helpful to know what resources are available to you if you are the victim of a criminal act. At the end of the day, an "ounce of prevention is worth a pound of cure," so the more knowledge you have, the more ammunition you possess, and the more likely you will have a positive outcome.

If you are traveling to Spain, the first thing you should pack is a copy of this book! The helpful information and tips contained in this volume will provide a great starting point for knowing what to do (and not to do!) when you arrive at your destination and will help ensure that you have a wonderful vacation or business trip unmarred by tangles with the law.

TABLE OF CONTENTS

INTRODUCTION

INTRODUCTION

As a practicing attorney for over 34 years, I have encountered numerous clients who travel often, but are unaware of the laws of the land they are traveling to.

Therefore, many years ago, I decided to write a series of books that would explain the laws of specific countries. My focus was to explain the laws that may affect travelers in a straightforward manner, without all of the legal language that is sometimes hard for even seasoned attorneys to understand.

About This Book

The aim of this book is simple. It provides you, the traveler, with a simple, easy to read book that will provide a basic legal guide that explains the law in the country that you are about to visit. It is not intended to educate you on ALL of the laws in a given country. The goal is to provide you with the details of the most common legal and safety issues faced by tourists and business travelers.

I have also provided context with background information on places not to visit, statistics on the country and prevention measures you should take to safeguard your legal and physical safety. Knowledge is a powerful thing and knowing how to stay out of trouble (or how to get out of it!) is important for everyone who travels.

This *Law of The Land/Spain* book simply helps you become more informed about your legal rights, responsibilities, and obligations in a wide range of subject areas.

Last, but not least, this book does NOT purport to offer legal advice. It does, however, provide the information you need to stay safe, follow the law and navigate around legal difficulties. However, if you do face legal difficulties, the information in this book will provide you with a starting point for solving the problem and obtaining legal assistance should it be required.

Hypotheticals Used Throughout This Book

From time to time throughout this book, I will explain the law to readers by using hypothetical scenarios. These hypotheticals will be marked by an icon that will be explained in further detail as you read on.

How This Book is Organized

CHAPTER 1: **About Spain.** This chapter will provide you with a brief overview about Spain and its history. It also addresses Visa requirements, monetary advice, and the best times to visit.

CHAPTER 2: **Customs.** This chapter will provide information on what to expect when entering Spain. It will also explain what restricted and prohibited items are when entering Spain along with custom's regulations.

CHAPTER 3: **Crime in Spain.** This chapter provides an overview of the history of crime in Spain and steps that Spain's officials have taken to curb the high rate of crime.

CHAPTER 4: **Criminal Law Violations.** This chapter will provide information on drug offenses, penalties, true events and questions and answers.

CHAPTER 5: **Alcohol-Related Offenses.** This chapter will provide key points regarding the sale, consumption, and regulations of alcohol use in Spain.

CHAPTER 6: **Firearm & Ammunition Offenses.** This chapter will provide key points regarding the possession of firearms and ammunition in Spain.

CHAPTER 7: **Prostitution.** This chapter provides an overview of the history of prostitution in Spain, laws and penalties, prostitution practices, sex trafficking, sex tourism, health in Spain, tips to avoid being hassled, a Law of the Land Hypothetical, and the current situation on prostitution in Spain.

CHAPTER 8: **LGBTQ.** This chapter will provide information regarding the acceptance of LGBTQ people in Spain and the laws surrounding homosexuality.

CHAPTER 9: **Sexually Motivated/Violent Crimes.** This chapter will provide an overview of sexually related crimes in Spain.

CHAPTER 10: **Arrested in Spain.** This chapter will provide information on what to do if you are arrested in Spain.

CHAPTER 11: **Jails vs. Prisons: Conditions & Culture.** This chapter will provide information on the conditions and culture of Spain's Jails and Prisons.

CHAPTER 12: **Helping a Friend or Relative Imprisoned in Spain.** This chapter will provide information on how you can assist a friend or relative imprisoned in Spain.

CHAPTER 13: **The Administration of Justice.** This chapter will provide information on Spain's Legal System.

CHAPTER 14: **Crime Victim Assistance.** This chapter will provide information on crime victim assistance along with providing safety tips.

CHAPTER 15: **Police.** This chapter will provide information on Spain's Police and how to report a crime.

CHAPTER 16: **How to Get Legal Help in Spain.** This chapter will provide information regarding how to obtain legal assistance for travelers to Spain.

CHAPTER 17: **Medical Facilities & Hospitals.** This chapter will provide information about how to obtain medical care while visiting Spain.

CHAPTER 18: **Driving in Spain.** This chapter will provide information on driving in Spain, traffic rules, and road safety tips.

CHAPTER 19: **Nude Beaches & Clothing-Optional Resorts.** This chapter will provide an overview of nude beaches and clothing-optional resorts in Spain, and the legality and safety of visiting nude beaches in Spain.

CHAPTER 20: **Unusual Laws.** This chapter will provide information on some Unusual Laws in Spain, and penalties and fines.

CHAPTER 21: **Traveling Safely.** This chapter will provide information on women traveling alone, crime prevention for families, safety notes for all travelers, and overall advice.

CHAPTER 22: **Tourist Taxation.** This chapter will provide information on taxes that tourists are required to pay in Spain.

CHAPTER 23: **Long-Term Stays.** This chapter will provide an overview of the consequences for overstaying your visit to Spain.

CHAPTER 24: **Civil Litigation.** This chapter will provide information about the civil litigation process in Spain.

CHAPTER 25: **Other Things to Know.** This chapter will provide information on the harassment of tourists, travel and safety, and other practical tips.

CHAPTER 26: **Quick Reference Guide.** This chapter is a quick way to get information. It is a condensed version of the chapters in this book.

Emergency/Important Contact Numbers in Spain

Useful Spanish Phrases

Glossary

Icons Used in this Book

What do those pictures throughout the book mean? See below:

 WARNING: This icon flags information about things you should **avoid** while visiting Spain. Heed the advice next to this icon to avoid legal perils.

 REMEMBER: This icon flags noteworthy information that you **shouldn't forget**.

 HELPFUL TIPS: This icon flags information that will help you when entering Spain, relates to a legal situation, or refers to resources available while visiting Spain.

 TECHNICAL INFORMATION: This icon flags technical aspects of the law. If you are faced with a legal problem, and you want to learn more about the law involved, this information can be helpful.

 **ADDITIONAL INFORMATION**: This icon points to the location of additional information available on the internet.

 **HYPOTHETICAL**: This icon points to hypothetical scenarios to illustrate possible legal problems and the outcome.

 **QUESTIONS**: This icon points to questions and answers throughout the book.

 **TRUE STORY**: This icon points to true events throughout the book.

Where to Go From Here

If you have a specific question about the law in Spain as it relates to a particular area, just turn to the chapter that addresses that issue, or turn to the Quick Reference Guide. You can also read the book from cover to cover to obtain a more comprehensive understanding of Spain's laws and resources available should you find yourself in a legal predicament while visiting.

 **Disclaimer:** While the recommendations in this book primarily address U.S. citizens, the information is relevant and applicable to citizens of any country.

ABOUT SPAIN

ABOUT SPAIN

About Spain

Spain is located in **Southwestern Europe** on the Iberian Peninsula, which it shares with Portugal. It is bordered to the northeast by France and Andorra, separated by the Pyrenees mountains, and surrounded by the Atlantic Ocean to the northwest and the Mediterranean Sea to the southeast. Spain also includes the **Balearic Islands** in the Mediterranean, the **Canary Islands** in the Atlantic Ocean, and two autonomous cities, **Ceuta** and **Melilla**, on the northern coast of Africa. Covering approximately 505,990 square kilometers (195,364 square miles), Spain is the **fourth-largest country in Europe**. As of 2023, Spain has a population of about **47.5 million people**, making it one of the most populous nations in the European Union.

Spain is well known for its rich culture, historic architecture, and diverse landscapes. The country offers everything from Mediterranean beaches and mountain ranges to sprawling countryside and bustling cities. It's internationally famous for **flamenco music and dance**, **bullfighting**, **delicious cuisine** (like tapas and paella), and **world-class wines**. Spain is also home to globally recognized artists such as **Pablo Picasso** and **Salvador Dalí**. With a vibrant lifestyle, countless festivals like **La Tomatina** and **Running of the Bulls**, and a strong emphasis on family and community, Spain is a top destination for travelers around the world.

Spain's history is marked by a blend of civilizations, including the Iberians, Celts, Romans, Visigoths, and Moors. After centuries of Muslim rule, Christian kingdoms gradually reclaimed the territory during the *Reconquista*, culminating in 1492 with the capture of Granada. That same year, Spain became a major global power following Christopher Columbus's first voyage to the Americas. Over the next few centuries, Spain built one of the largest empires in history, spanning much of the Americas, parts of Europe, Africa, and Asia. The Spanish Empire declined in the 19th century, with most of its colonies gaining independence. In the 20th century, Spain experienced a brutal civil war (1936–1939), which led to a dictatorship under Francisco Franco. Following Franco's death in **1975**, Spain transitioned to a **democracy** and became a **parliamentary constitutional monarchy**. Today, it is a member of the European Union, NATO, and the United Nations, and it enjoys political stability and a high quality of life.

The Capital

Madrid, the capital of Spain, is located in the center of the country on the Meseta Central, a high plateau that dominates central Spain. As the **largest city** in the country, Madrid is the political, economic, and cultural heart of Spain. It is home to the Spanish royal family and the national government. Known for its elegant boulevards, bustling plazas, and expansive parks such as El Retiro, Madrid blends modern infrastructure with rich history.

Cultural landmarks include the **Prado Museum**, the **Royal Palace**, and **Plaza Mayor**, all of which reflect the city's historical and artistic importance. Madrid also boasts a lively nightlife, a celebrated culinary scene, and a passion for sports—especially **soccer**—with **Real Madrid** and **Atlético Madrid** being two of Europe's top clubs. Despite its urban energy, Madrid retains a relaxed charm, with traditions and modernity existing side by side.

The People

The people of Spain, known as Spaniards, are a diverse population characterized by **regional identities and languages**. Spain is composed of **17**

autonomous communities, each with its own customs and traditions, contributing to the country's rich cultural tapestry.

The Spanish are known for their warmth, strong sense of family, and a laid-back approach to life—reflected in their love of social gatherings, long meals, and afternoon siestas. Spanish culture places a high value on personal relationships and community. Celebrations and festivals are central to life, with events such as Semana Santa (Holy Week) and Feria de Abril in Seville drawing large crowds. Traditional music and dance— especially flamenco in Andalusia—are expressions of regional pride. While urban areas are fast-paced and cosmopolitan, rural communities maintain centuries-old customs and a slower pace of life.

Language

The official language of Spain is **Spanish**, also known as **Castilian** (*Castellano*), which is spoken nationwide. However, several regions have co-official languages, reflecting the country's linguistic diversity. These include **Catalan** in Catalonia and the Balearic Islands, **Galician** in Galicia, and **Basque** (*Euskara*) in the Basque Country and parts of Navarre.

Many Spaniards are bilingual, particularly in regions with strong local identities. Spanish spoken in Spain differs slightly in pronunciation and vocabulary from Latin American Spanish, but it is mutually intelligible. English is commonly taught in schools and increasingly used in tourist areas, though proficiency levels vary.

Religion

Spain is a historically Catholic country, and **Roman Catholicism** has played a central role in shaping its history, architecture, and traditions. Today, about 58-65 percent of Spaniards identify as Roman Catholic, though active participation in religious practices has declined in recent decades, especially among younger generations.

Spain is **officially a secular state with freedom of religion**. There are growing communities of Muslims, Protestants, Jews, Buddhists, and non-religious individuals. Important Catholic traditions remain prominent, especially during holidays like Easter and Christmas, and many Spanish towns and cities still celebrate their patron saints with local festivals and processions.

Affordability

Spain is considered an **affordable European destination**, especially compared to northern and western European countries. The cost of living varies by region. Madrid and Barcelona tend to be more expensive, while smaller cities and rural areas offer more budget-friendly options.

Accommodation ranges from luxury hotels and boutique stays to hostels and vacation rentals. A night in a mid-range hotel can cost between €60 to €100 (about US$65 to $110), while budget hostels or guesthouses might be as low as €20 to €30 (US$22 to $33) per night. Airbnb and other short-term rentals are also widely available and offer flexible pricing.

Food is relatively inexpensive, especially if you dine at local tapas bars or neighborhood cafes. A good meal at a casual restaurant may cost around €10 to €15 (US$11 to $16), and a cup of coffee usually runs €1.50 to €2.50 (US$1.65 to $2.75). Dining at high-end restaurants can be more expensive but still generally offers better value than in the U.S. or UK.

Transportation is efficient and affordable. Metro or bus tickets in cities typically cost €1.50 to €2 (US$1.65 to $2.20), while monthly public transit passes range from €35 to €55 (US$38 to $60) depending on the city. Spain's **high-speed trains (AVE)** offer fast travel between major cities, though tickets can range from €30 to over €100 (US$33 to $110), depending on the route and how early you book.

Many of **Spain's attractions** are either free or low-cost. Public beaches, city parks, and historical plazas are often open to all. Entrance to major museums like the Prado or Reina Sofía in Madrid is typically around €15 (US$16.50), and many offer free hours on select days. Guided tours, flamenco shows, and excursions may range from €25 to €70 (US$27 to $77).

Spain, the Basics

How to Get There?

Spain is one of the most accessible destinations in Europe, well-connected by air to cities across North America, Latin America, Asia, and other parts of Europe. It has multiple international airports with direct flights arriving daily from major global hubs. Spain is served by a wide range of full-service and budget airlines, making travel options flexible and often affordable, depending on the season and departure location. Major airports in Spain include:

1. **Madrid-Barajas Adolfo Suárez Airport (MAD):** Located in the capital city of Madrid, MAD is the largest and busiest airport in Spain. It serves as a major international gateway, especially for flights from North and South America, Europe, and Asia. The airport is also a key hub for Iberia, Spain's flagship airline.

2. **Barcelona-El Prat Airport (BCN):** This is Spain's second-busiest airport and the main international gateway to Catalonia. It handles numerous transatlantic and intra-European flights and is a major hub for Vueling Airlines and a key base for Ryanair and Iberia.

3. **Málaga-Costa del Sol Airport (AGP):** Serving southern Spain and the Costa del Sol region, Málaga is one of the most popular destinations for tourists, especially from the UK, Germany, and Scandinavia. It offers many low-cost and seasonal flights.

4. **Palma de Mallorca Airport (PMI):** Located in the Balearic Islands, this airport is a major hub for holiday travelers from Europe, particularly during the summer months.

5. **Alicante-Elche Airport (ALC):** Another important airport along Spain's Mediterranean coast, popular with travelers heading to beach resorts. It sees heavy seasonal traffic from across Europe.

6. **Gran Canaria Airport (LPA) and Tenerife South Airport (TFS):** These airports serve the Canary Islands, located off the northwest coast of Africa. Both handle a significant volume of international flights, especially from European cities.

Spain is served by a wide range of international and regional airlines, making it highly accessible from across the globe. **Iberia**, Spain's national carrier and a member of the Oneworld alliance, offers direct flights from major U.S. cities such as New York, Miami, and Chicago, as well as extensive connections throughout Latin America and Europe. **American Airlines** also provides direct routes to Madrid and Barcelona from U.S. hubs like New York (JFK), Miami (MIA), and Dallas (DFW). **Delta Airlines** operates transatlantic flights from cities such as New York and Atlanta to both Madrid and Barcelona, while **United Airlines** serves routes from Newark (EWR), Washington D.C., and Chicago.

For those flying from other parts of the world, **Air France** and **KLM** offer convenient connecting flights to Spanish cities via Paris and Amsterdam respectively. **British Airways** links Spain to North America and global destinations through its London hub, and **Lufthansa** flies into Spain from Frankfurt and Munich, often with U.S. connections. For budget-conscious travelers, low-cost carriers like **Vueling**, **Ryanair**, and **EasyJet** offer frequent and affordable flights from numerous European cities, making them ideal for short-haul travel and regional connections within Europe.

When to Visit?

Spain offers a wide range of experiences year-round, but the best time to visit depends on what you're looking for—whether it's pleasant weather, fewer crowds, or specific cultural events.

Weather-wise, the most favorable time to visit Spain is **during the spring (April to June)** and **fall (September to early November)**. During these months, the weather is typically warm and sunny, but not excessively hot, making it ideal for sightseeing, exploring cities like Madrid and Barcelona, or enjoying the countryside and coastlines. Summer (July and August) can be very hot, especially in inland areas like Seville or Madrid, with temperatures often exceeding 35°C (95°F). However, coastal regions and the islands offer refreshing sea breezes, making summer a good time for beach holidays. Winter (December to February) is generally mild in the south but much cooler in the north and central regions. It's also the best season for snow sports in the Pyrenees and Sierra Nevada.

Crowd-wise, **peak travel season** runs from **June to August**, when schools are out and tourists from across Europe flock to Spain. Prices for flights and accommodation can rise significantly during this time, especially in popular destinations like Barcelona, Ibiza, and the Costa del Sol. Spring and fall are considered shoulder seasons, offering fewer crowds and better rates, while still enjoying great weather. **Winter** is the **least crowded season**, except around Christmas and New Year's, when holiday tourism picks up, especially in major cities and festive regions.

Activities-wise, spring and fall are perfect for walking tours, wine tasting, cultural events, and outdoor adventures in both cities and nature. Summer is ideal for beachgoers, water sports enthusiasts, and nightlife lovers, especially on islands like Ibiza and Mallorca. Winter is the season for skiing in mountain resorts and enjoying cozy city breaks with fewer tourists. Spain's diverse climate means there's always something to enjoy, from sunbathing on the Mediterranean coast to hiking in the Basque Country or skiing in Granada.

If you're drawn to **festivals**, Spain has a rich calendar of cultural events worth timing your trip around. **Semana Santa** (Holy Week), held in **March or April**, features dramatic religious processions throughout the country, especially in Seville and Málaga. **La Feria de Abril** (April Fair) in Seville showcases Andalusian culture with flamenco, food, and parades. **San Fermín** (Running of the Bulls) takes place in Pamplona every **July** and draws thrill-seekers and spectators from around the world. In August, **La Tomatina** in Buñol offers the world's biggest tomato fight. **Fiesta Nacional de España** (October 12) and local **harvest festivals** throughout the fall also provide opportunities to experience Spain's rich traditions and regional cuisines. Whether you want to dance in the streets or immerse yourself in history and local life, there's always something happening in Spain.

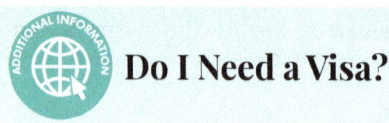

Do I Need a Visa?

Whether you need a visa to visit Spain depends on your nationality and the purpose of your visit. For many travelers, particularly those from the United States, Canada, the United Kingdom, Australia, and most countries within the European Union, a visa is **not required** for short stays of up to **90 days** within a **180-day period** for tourism, business, or family visits. However, your passport must be valid for at least **three months** beyond your planned date of departure from the Schengen Area, and it should have been issued within the last ten years.

Spain is part of the **Schengen Area,** which means that once you enter Spain, you can also travel freely to other Schengen countries without additional border checks. **Starting in 2025,** travelers from visa-exempt countries will need to apply for **ETIAS (European Travel Information and Authorization System),** an electronic travel authorization that costs about **€7** (approximately US$7.50) and is valid for three years or until your passport expires.

If you are from a country that is **not visa-exempt,** you'll need to apply for a **Schengen visa** before arriving in Spain. This visa allows travel within the Schengen Zone and must be obtained from the Spanish consulate or embassy in your home country. Processing fees for a short-term visa are usually around **€80** (about US$86) for adults, with discounted rates for children and other eligible groups.

For stays longer than 90 days, or if you're traveling for work, study, or residence purposes, you will need to apply for a **long-stay national visa,** which involves additional documentation and approval through the Spanish consulate (discussed in Chapter 23).

It's always best to check with the **nearest Spanish consulate or embassy** for the most accurate and updated entry requirements based on your nationality and the purpose of your visit.

How to Get Around

Getting around Spain is convenient and efficient, thanks to its well-developed transportation infrastructure. For tourists, the most popular and reliable option for long-distance travel is the **train system**, particularly the high-speed **AVE trains**, which connect major cities like **Madrid**, **Barcelona**, **Seville**, **Valencia**, and **Málaga**. These trains are fast, comfortable, and scenic, though prices can vary. Booking in advance often secures better deals (tickets can range from **US$25 to $120**, depending on distance and how early you book).

For shorter trips or local travel, **metro systems** in cities like **Madrid**, **Barcelona**, and **Valencia** offer an affordable and efficient way to get around. Single metro tickets typically cost around €1.50 to €2.50 (US$1.60 to $2.70), and multi-day or travel cards can offer better value for longer stays. **City buses** and **trams** are also widely available and easy to use.

Taxis are plentiful and metered in most cities, but **Uber**, **Cabify**, and **Bolt** are also available in many urban areas, often providing a more transparent fare structure. Prices vary by city and distance but tend to be reasonable (for example, a 15-minute Uber ride in Madrid might cost around **US$10 to $15**).

If you're planning to explore the countryside or more remote regions like Andalusia, Galicia, or the Basque Country, **renting a car** can be a great option for flexibility. Rental prices start at about €25 to €40 (US$27 to $43) per day, but keep in mind that city traffic and parking can be challenging in older urban centers.

For budget-conscious travelers, **long-distance buses**, such as **ALSA** and **Avanza**, offer extensive coverage across Spain and into neighboring countries. They're slower than trains but significantly cheaper—fares for intercity routes can be as low as **US$10 to $20**.

In coastal towns and islands like Ibiza, Mallorca, or Tenerife, **ferries** and **bike rentals** are popular options. Many tourist spots also offer **guided walking tours**, electric scooters, and **hop-on-hop-off buses** for convenient sightseeing. Depending on your itinerary, Spain offers a flexible mix of modern transit options to suit any travel style.

Monetary Advice

The official currency of Spain is the **euro** (**EUR**). Exchange rates fluctuate, but typically, **US$1 equals around €0.90 to €0.95**, depending on market conditions. You can exchange currency at banks, exchange bureaus, and at the airport, though airport rates tend to be less favorable. **ATMs** are widely available throughout Spain and usually offer competitive exchange rates with minimal fees, especially if you use a debit card that waives foreign transaction charges.

Credit and debit cards are widely accepted in Spain, especially in urban areas, hotels, restaurants, shops, and even many taxis. **Visa and Mastercard** are the most commonly used, while **American Express** is accepted at some establishments, though less frequently. It's always a good idea to carry a small amount of cash for smaller purchases, tips, or places that don't accept cards (like small cafés or rural shops). Also, notify your bank before traveling to avoid any security holds on your card abroad.

Spain uses only euros; **U.S. dollars or other foreign currencies are generally not accepted**, so you'll need to exchange or withdraw euros for most transactions. Some major tourist hubs may offer price listings in dollars for convenience, but payment will still be required in euros.

In Spain, bargaining is **not common**, especially in retail stores or restaurants where prices are fixed. However, in **open-air markets** or when purchasing **handicrafts and souvenirs** from street vendors, there might be some room for light, respectful negotiation—though it's not expected or widespread.

Also bear in mind that **tipping** in Spain is more **modest** compared to North America. At restaurants, tipping is appreciated but not obligatory—**leaving 5–10 percent** is typical for good service, especially in tourist areas. In cafés or bars, it's common to round up the bill or leave small change. **Hotel staff** such as housekeepers and bellhops may be tipped €1 to €2 (US$1.10 to $2.20) per day or per bag. **Taxi drivers** do not expect tips, but rounding up the fare is customary. For **tour guides**, a **tip of €5 to €10** (US$5.50 to $11) is appreciated for excellent service. Carrying small euro bills and coins is helpful for tipping and minor purchases.

Spanish Hospitality

Spanish hospitality is deeply rooted in the country's **rich traditions, strong family values**, and **vibrant social culture.** Spain is widely known for its **warm, expressive**, and **friendly** people who take pride in welcoming visitors with open arms. Whether you're strolling through a bustling city like Madrid or relaxing in a small village in Andalusia, you're likely to be greeted with genuine smiles, cheerful conversation, and a sense of inclusion that makes you feel like part of the community.

Hospitality in Spain is often shown through **sharing food, conversation**, and **time.** Meals are a central part of Spanish social life, and it's not unusual to be invited to join locals for tapas, a coffee, or even a full home-cooked meal. Hosts are typically generous and enjoy engaging guests in spirited discussions over wine or traditional dishes like **paella** or **jamón ibérico.** Even in a casual setting, offering visitors something to eat or drink is a customary gesture of warmth and respect.

Politeness and respect are important in Spanish culture, but social interactions tend to be relaxed and informal. A friendly *"hola"* (hello), *"gracias"* (thank you), or *"por favor"* (please) goes a long way. When meeting someone, a **handshake** is common, though close friends and acquaintances often greet with a kiss on both cheeks (starting with the right cheek). Maintaining eye contact during conversation shows attentiveness and sincerity, which is appreciated. On the flip side, interrupting someone, speaking too loudly in quiet settings (like churches), or failing to greet people when entering a room or shop may be viewed as impolite.

While Spaniards are often forgiving of cultural differences, **making an effort to learn a few Spanish phrases,** respecting local customs, and showing interest in the culture will be warmly received. To show respect as a visitor, **embrace the local rhythm of life**—including late meals, afternoon siestas in some regions, and the importance of family and community gatherings. Participating in cultural events, trying local cuisine, and being open to conversation—even if your Spanish isn't perfect—are excellent ways to connect. Simply being curious, courteous, and open-minded will ensure you experience the best of Spanish hospitality.

CHAPTER 2
CUSTOMS

- Travelers Entering Spain
- Customs Entitlements and Monetary Restrictions
- Restricted and Prohibited Items
- Five Practical Tips to Know Before You Go

CHAPTER 2

CUSTOMS

Travelers Entering Spain[1]

When traveling to Spain, visitors must have a **valid passport** with at least **three to six months of validity** remaining beyond their planned departure date. **Citizens from the United States, Canada, the UK**, and **most EU countries do not need a visa for short visits of up to 90 days within a 180-day period**, as Spain is part of the **Schengen Area**. However, travelers must not overstay this limit, and those from countries outside the visa waiver list should apply for a **Schengen visa** in advance through their nearest Spanish consulate or embassy.

Upon arrival in Spain, travelers will go through standard **immigration and customs procedures**. At immigration, you'll need to present your passport, and you may be asked to show proof of your accommodation, a return or onward flight ticket, and evidence of sufficient funds for your stay.

Once you pass through immigration, you'll proceed to baggage claim and then customs. **Spain generally doesn't require declarations unless you're bringing in restricted or high-value goods**, but there are limits on items like tobacco, alcohol, and cash (see below). Customs checks are usually swift, especially for travelers arriving from within the EU, but

---

1   https://genuineandalusia.com/spain-travel-advisory-2025

they can take longer at major international airports like Madrid-Barajas (MAD) or Barcelona-El Prat (BCN), especially during peak hours.

After collecting your luggage, you'll find airport services such as **currency exchange, SIM card kiosks, car rental desks, and transportation options**, including official taxis, ride-hailing apps (like Uber, Cabify, or Bolt in select cities), and metro or train connections, depending on the airport. Taxis in Spain are metered, and prices are regulated, but always make sure the meter is running or ask about the fare if traveling long-distance.

Although many people in the tourism industry speak English, **Spanish is the official language**, so learning a few basic phrases like "*hola*" (hello) or "*gracias*" (thank you) can go a long way in making connections with locals.

 To stay updated on travel requirements and safety guidelines, it's highly recommended to check the **U.S. Department of State's travel website** at **travel.state.gov** or the **official Spain tourism portal** at **spain.info**. These sources offer reliable information about entry conditions, regional advisories, health alerts, and helpful tips for travelers planning their Spanish adventure

Customs Entitlements and Monetary Restrictions[2]

When entering Spain, there are specific customs entitlements and monetary restrictions that travelers should be aware of to ensure a smooth arrival. Here's what you need to know about what you can and cannot bring into the country:

---

2   https://en.tripmydream.com/spain/custom

Currency:

Spain, as part of the European Union, allows travelers to bring in foreign currency without restriction. However, if you're carrying **€10,000 or more (or the equivalent in other currencies)**—whether in cash, checks, or money orders—you must **declare it to customs** upon arrival. This regulation applies to all travelers, regardless of nationality, and is aimed at preventing illegal financial activity. Failure to declare amounts over this threshold may result in fines or the confiscation of the funds.[3]

Permitted Items:

Personal belongings such as clothing, toiletries, cameras, phones, laptops, and other items for individual use are allowed and do not need to be declared if they are clearly for personal travel purposes.

Duty-Free Allowances (for non-EU arrivals): Travelers arriving from non-EU countries can bring the following items into Spain without paying customs duties, provided they are for personal use:

Alcohol:

- 1 liter of spirits over 22 percent alcohol, or
- 2 liters of alcoholic beverages under 22 percent (e.g., wine or liqueurs),
- Plus 4 liters of still wine and 16 liters of beer.

Tobacco:

- 200 cigarettes, or
- 100 cigarillos, or
- 50 cigars, or
- 250g of smoking tobacco.

---

3   https://www.aena.es/en/passengers/baggage-controls/customs-vat-refund/circulation-goods-money.html

Other Goods:

- Non-alcohol and non-tobacco goods up to a value of €430 (around US$485) **for air and sea travelers** or €300 (around US$338) for **land travelers.** For travelers under 15 years old, the allowance is €150 (around US$170).

Gifts and Souvenirs: Gifts and souvenirs brought into Spain are permitted as long as they fall within the above value limits and are clearly not intended for resale. If you're carrying larger quantities of items such as clothing, electronics, or cosmetics, you may be questioned by customs officials.

Food: Travelers should be cautious about bringing food into Spain. **Animal-based products** such as meat, dairy, or anything made from them are strictly **prohibited from non-EU countries** due to health and safety regulations. **Packaged snacks, candies, and non-perishable items** may be allowed in small quantities for personal use, but it's advisable to check updated guidelines or avoid bringing food altogether.

Electronics and Personal Devices: Personal electronics like phones, laptops, and cameras are allowed for individual use. However, bringing in **multiple devices** of the same type or high-value items in bulk may suggest commercial intent and could lead to customs duties or confiscation.

Cosmetics and Toiletries: Cosmetics and toiletries are permitted for personal use in travel-sized amounts. Large quantities may raise suspicion about commercial purposes and could be subject to customs review.

To ensure a smooth entry into Spain, it's important to **declare any large amounts of currency, avoid bringing restricted goods,** and **keep all personal-use items in reasonable quantities.** For the most up-to-date customs and entry information, visit Spain's **Tax and Customs Agency** website at **agenciatributaria.es.**

 ## Restricted and Prohibited Items

Spain has specific rules regarding **prohibited** and **restricted items** that travelers should be aware of when entering the country. Familiarizing yourself with these guidelines will help avoid complications at customs and ensure that you comply with local laws.

Prohibited Items include:

- **Illegal drugs and narcotics:** The possession, use, or trafficking of any illegal drugs, including marijuana, is strictly prohibited in Spain. Even small amounts can result in severe penalties, including fines, arrest, and imprisonment.

- **Firearms, ammunition, and explosives:** These items are generally banned, unless you have a special permit. Weapons of any kind, including knives and other dangerous objects, are not allowed unless specifically authorized by law.

- **Counterfeit goods:** The importation of counterfeit products, including fake clothing, shoes, handbags, electronics, and accessories, is prohibited. Customs officers will confiscate counterfeit items, and you could face legal consequences.

- **Endangered species products:** Spain enforces strict rules against the import of products made from endangered species. This includes items like ivory, certain types of leather, and animal skins, which are not allowed into the country. Products such as jewelry, handbags, and clothing made from these materials are also prohibited.

- **Pornographic material:** Importing or possessing pornographic material is illegal in Spain, and such items will be seized if found.

- **Fresh fruits, vegetables, and plants:** These items are restricted because they can carry pests and diseases that pose risks to local ecosystems and agriculture. Some plant products may require special permits for import.

Restricted Items include:

- **Agricultural products:** Certain agricultural products, including meats, dairy, and fresh food, may be subject to inspection or prohibition. If allowed, some may require specific permits for entry.

- **Pets:** While pets, such as dogs and cats, are allowed, they must meet health certification requirements, including vaccinations, such as rabies, before being imported. Exotic animals and wildlife are subject to additional restrictions and may require special permits.

- **Medications:** Prescription medications for personal use are generally allowed, but some may be restricted. If your medication contains controlled substances, you may need to provide supporting documentation, such as a doctor's prescription or a health certificate.

- **Cultural artifacts and antiquities:** Spain, like many countries, places restrictions on the import and export of cultural artifacts and antiquities to protect its national heritage.

- **Alcohol and tobacco:** While you are allowed to bring a reasonable amount of alcohol and tobacco for personal use, excessive quantities may be subject to customs duties.

Bringing restricted or prohibited items into Spain can lead to **severe penalties.** Customs officers may seize the items, and you could face fines, legal action, or even arrest, depending on the severity of the offense. If caught with counterfeit goods or products made from endangered species, the items will be confiscated, and you may face additional legal consequences. For items like unlicensed pharmaceuticals or agricultural products, you may be required to pay penalties or have the goods returned or destroyed.

 It is crucial to check the regulations and ensure you have the proper documentation for any restricted items before traveling to Spain. For more detailed information on prohibited and restricted items, you can visit Spain's official **Tax and Customs Agency** website at **agenciatributaria.es.**

 # Five Practical Tips to Know Before You Go

1. In many parts of Spain, especially smaller towns, a midday break—or *siesta*—is still common. Shops and restaurants may close between 2:00PM and 5:00PM, so plan accordingly and take the time to relax like the locals.

2. Spaniards eat and socialize later than many travelers are used to. Lunch is typically around 2:00PM and dinner often starts after 9:00PM. Adjusting to this schedule helps you experience local life more authentically.

3. People in Spain generally dress well, even casually. Avoid wearing gym clothes or flip-flops outside of beaches or workouts. Dress modestly when visiting religious sites to show respect.

4. English is spoken in tourist areas but using basic Spanish shows respect and goes a long way in everyday interactions. (See *Useful Spanish Phrases* at the end of the book.)

5. Greetings are important. A simple *hola* when entering a shop is polite. In social settings, two cheek kisses are common, while handshakes are used in formal situations. Knowing this helps make a good impression.

CRIME IN SPAIN

CHAPTER 3

CRIME IN SPAIN

Overview

Spain is widely regarded as a **low-crime country**, with a crime rate lower than in many other European countries. The homicide rate is notably low and stable, recorded at 0.68 incidents per 100,000 inhabitants in 2022, which is under the European Union average.[4]

Petty crimes such as pickpocketing, especially in tourist-heavy areas like Barcelona and Madrid, are the most commonly reported offenses. Several factors contribute to crime in Spain. Economic disparities and youth unemployment, particularly in certain regions, can influence property crimes. Tourism is also a significant factor, as large crowds in popular destinations provide opportunities for theft and scams. Additionally, organized crime, including drug trafficking and smuggling, has some presence, particularly in port cities and coastal areas.

Over the years, crime trends in Spain have shown a **general decline**. Data from the past two decades indicates a steady drop in overall crime rates, especially violent crime. In recent years, while some specific crimes like cybercrime and domestic violence have seen slight increases, the broader trend continues to show stability or gradual improvement. Spanish law enforcement agencies have also increased digital crime prevention

---

4   https://www.statista.com/topics/12673/crime-in-spain/

measures, and public safety initiatives have helped maintain low crime levels in many communities.

Crime Hotspots in Spain

Certain areas in Spain are known for higher crime rates, primarily due to their popularity with tourists. Major cities like **Barcelona** and **Madrid** are the most notable crime hotspots, particularly for **non-violent offenses** such as pickpocketing, bag snatching, and scams. Barcelona, in particular, consistently ranks as one of the top European cities for petty theft, especially in areas like **Las Ramblas**, the **Gothic Quarter**, and **near major transport hubs**. Other regions like the **Costa del Sol** and **Valencia** also report higher crime rates during peak tourist seasons, though violent crime remains relatively rare.

For up-to-date travel safety information, the **U.S. Department of State** regularly publishes advisories for Spain on its official website: **travel.state.gov/**. Spain is typically rated at **Level 2: Exercise Increased Caution**, mainly due to the risk of petty crime in tourist areas. However, when compared internationally, particularly to the United States, Spain is considerably safer. According to various global crime indices, Spain has a significantly lower violent crime rate than the U.S., including lower rates of homicide and gun-related violence. The U.S. sees more frequent violent incidents and gun-related crimes, while Spain's issues are mostly limited to non-violent theft and fraud in urban and tourist-dense areas.

 Before traveling, it's always a good idea to check **official travel advisories** from your home country.

Crime Statistics

The Global Peace Index ranks Spain 32nd out of 163 countries and 23rd among European countries in 2023, highlighting its overall societal safety and security. Public perception also supports this assessment: about 80 percent of people feel safe walking alone at night in Spain.[5]

As mentioned above, the most common and widespread types of crime are non-violent offenses, particularly **petty theft**, **pickpocketing**, **bag snatching**, and **scams** targeting tourists. These crimes are prevalent in busy public areas, such as metro stations, tourist attractions, markets, and nightlife districts. In larger cities like Barcelona, Madrid, and Seville, incidents of phone theft and distraction-based scams are especially frequent.

Compared to global and regional averages, Spain fares well. According to international crime indices, Spain has lower rates of **violent crime** and **homicide** than the global average and is notably safer than many countries in the Americas and parts of Eastern Europe. In Western Europe, it ranks among the safer nations in terms of violent crime, though its rate of non-violent theft is slightly higher due to its large influx of tourists.

Spanish law enforcement is generally viewed as professional and effective. While isolated cases of corruption have occurred, overall confidence in police services is relatively high, particularly in urban centers. Spain's national police and Guardia Civil have implemented modern crime-prevention tools, including surveillance and digital crime units, helping keep violent crime rates low and responding quickly to organized criminal activity.

Crimes impacting tourists are mainly opportunistic thefts and violent incidents involving tourists are rare.

---

5   https://www.expatica.com/es/living/gov-law-admin/
     crime-in-spain-106655/

Quick Safety Tips

- Pickpockets target busy places like metros, markets, and tourist spots; keep bags zipped and valuables close.

- Use a crossbody bag—it's harder to snatch and easier to keep in sight than backpacks or shoulder bags.

- Avoid displaying valuables because flashing phones, jewelry, or large amounts of cash can attract thieves.

- Be cautious of distractions—scams often involve someone spilling something or asking for help—don't let your guard down.

- Stick to registered taxi services or ride-sharing apps like Uber or Cabify to avoid unlicensed drivers.

CRIMINAL LAW VIOLATIONS

CHAPTER 4

CRIMINAL LAW VIOLATIONS

Marijuana and Other Drugs in Spain[6]

Spain has a long-standing and nuanced relationship with cannabis. Historically, cannabis has been socially tolerated more than other drugs, especially in private settings. Over time, certain regions like Catalonia and the Basque Country have developed particularly permissive attitudes toward cannabis use.

Medical marijuana in Spain is **partially legal**. In 2022, the government approved regulated use of medical cannabis, but the program is still developing and not widely accessible. Patients still face challenges accessing legal cannabis-based treatments, and much of the current medical use is supported by private import or through informal channels, pending further regulation. **Recreational marijuana**, on the other hand, is **decriminalized for personal use in private**, meaning individuals can grow small amounts for personal consumption at home. However, **public consumption or possession remains illegal** and subject to fines.

One distinctive feature in Spain is the existence of **cannabis social clubs**. These are private, non-profit associations where members collectively grow and share cannabis. While not officially legal, they are tolerated under privacy laws, provided they follow **strict guidelines**: these clubs

---

6   https://sensiseeds.com/en/blog/countries/
    cannabis-in-spain-laws-use-history/

must operate as non-profits, limit access to registered adult members, and keep cultivation quantities aligned with personal use. Clubs that are found to be selling to non-members or operating like businesses risk being shut down or prosecuted. The status of these clubs varies depending on the region, with some local governments showing more tolerance than others, but by and large the authorities have begun cracking down on clubs that appear to operate commercially or beyond the legal gray zone as current laws maintain a firm stance against public consumption or large-scale cultivation. While private use is decriminalized, the sale and trafficking of marijuana are still considered criminal offenses and can lead to imprisonment.

Synthetic cannabinoids are **banned** in Spain. These substances are treated as dangerous, and their possession, sale, or manufacture is strictly prohibited, with legal consequences similar to those for other hard drugs. For **other substances**, Spain differentiates clearly between personal use and trafficking. While **personal possession** of even hard drugs like ecstasy, heroin, or methamphetamines **won't lead to jail time if the quantity is small and for personal use**, any evidence of **distribution or intent to sell** triggers **criminal prosecution**. Border areas and ports, especially in southern Spain, are more closely monitored due to smuggling activities, particularly involving drugs from North Africa.

Law enforcement is generally viewed as fair and professional, though some regions may vary in the consistency of enforcement. Police regularly conduct patrols in tourist areas and nightlife districts to deter drug-related offenses and often issue on-the-spot fines for public consumption. Overall, the combination of permissive private use and strong public control aims to balance personal freedom with public safety.

Penalties[7]

In Spain, the penalties for drug-related offenses depend on whether the activity involves personal use or distribution. For **marijuana**, private

---

7   https://criminallawyersmarbella.com/
    drug-related-crimes-in-spain-penalties-and-legal-defense/

use and cultivation for personal consumption are decriminalized. This means that individuals are not prosecuted criminally if they use or grow cannabis discreetly at home and in small quantities. However, if someone is caught **using or possessing marijuana in public**, they can face **administrative fines** ranging from **€601 to €30,000** (approximately US$640 to $32,000), and the substance will be confiscated. If home cultivation exceeds what is considered for personal use or is visible from public spaces, it may be treated as intent to distribute, which turns the act into a **criminal offense**.

Cannabis Social Clubs exist in a legal gray area. They are tolerated if operated non-commercially and within strict guidelines. If a club is found **distributing cannabis for profit** or **violating membership regulations**, those responsible may be prosecuted for trafficking, with prison sentences ranging from one to three years and potential fines.

Trafficking or large-scale cultivation of marijuana is considered a **serious criminal offense** in Spain. Sentences usually range from three to **six years in prison, and can extend to nine years in aggravated cases**, such as involving minors, being near schools, or operating as part of a criminal organization. Fines in trafficking cases are typically tied to the street value of the drugs involved and can be substantial.

Synthetic cannabinoids are fully illegal. Possession, sale, or production of these substances is treated with the same severity as that of hard drugs. If the amount possessed suggests intent to distribute, the offender may face **prison terms between three and nine years**, depending on the scale and circumstances of the offense.

For other **illicit substances** like cocaine, heroin, ecstasy, and methamphetamines, Spanish law also distinguishes between personal use and trafficking. **Small amounts for personal use are decriminalized** if used in private. However, **public possession results in administrative fines**, again ranging from **€601 to €30,000** (US$640 to $32,000). If **trafficking or intent to sell** is proven, **criminal charges** apply, with prison sentences ranging from **three to nine years** and possibly longer for repeat offenders or cases involving aggravating factors.

While Spain takes a relatively lenient stance on private, personal drug use—especially cannabis—it imposes harsh penalties for public possession, trafficking, or large-scale operations, with strict enforcement by law enforcement and the judicial system.

Prescription Medication

Travelers to Spain are generally allowed to bring prescription medication for personal use, but there are rules and limitations to be aware of. If you're bringing medication with you, especially controlled substances, it's important to carry **a copy of the prescription** and a **doctor's note** explaining the medical need. The quantity of the medication should be relative to the duration of your stay; however, travelers are typically permitted to bring **up to a three-month supply** for personal use. The documentation should include your name, the medication's name, dosage, and the prescribing doctor's details. Keeping medications in their **original packaging** with clear labeling is also recommended.[8]

Spain follows EU regulations, so medications considered **controlled substances**—such as opioids, stimulants (like those for ADHD), or certain anxiety medications—may require **prior authorization** from the Spanish health authorities. In such cases, travelers are advised to contact the Spanish consulate before traveling to ensure they meet entry requirements.

Over-the-counter (OTC) medications like pain relievers or antihistamines can usually be brought in small, personal-use quantities without issue. However, some medications that are sold over-the-counter in other countries may be considered prescription-only or even restricted in Spain. For example, products containing **codeine** or **pseudoephedrine** can raise red flags and may be confiscated or result in questions at customs if brought in large amounts or without documentation.

8   https://www.healthplanspain.com/blog/expat-tips/1587-can-you-bring-prescription-medicines-into-spain.html

Bringing in large quantities of medication, failing to declare controlled substances, or lacking appropriate documentation can lead to confiscation of the medication, fines, or in more serious cases, legal repercussions. In rare situations involving undeclared narcotic medications or suspicion of trafficking, travelers could face criminal investigation. If you're unsure whether your medication is allowed, check with the **Spanish Agency of Medicines and Medical Devices (AEMPS)** or your local Spanish consulate before your trip.

It's important to note that **shipping medications by mail to Spain is prohibited**. Therefore, ensure you bring all necessary medications with you in your carry-on luggage to avoid any issues.

For further information and to ensure you have the most current guidelines, consult the official Spanish customs regulations at **spain.info/en/travel-tips/customs-regulations/** and the U.S. Embassy website at **es.usembassy.gov/medical-assistance/**.

General Questions

1. *Is cannabis legal in Spain?* **No**. Cannabis is **not legal** in Spain, but it is **decriminalized** for personal use in private spaces. This means you won't face criminal charges for consuming or growing small amounts for personal use at home, as long as it's not visible from public areas. However, **buying, selling, or using cannabis in public is illegal** and can result in hefty fines.

2. *Where can I legally purchase marijuana in Spain?* You can't legally buy marijuana in shops in Spain. However, **Cannabis Social Clubs** operate in a legal gray area where **registered adult members** can access cannabis for personal use. These clubs are private, non-profit, and usually **not open to tourists** or walk-ins—you typically need to be a resident or stay long-term. Buying on the street is illegal and can result in fines or criminal charges.

3. *Can I have marijuana on my person or in hotel room in Spain?* **Yes.** In Spain, possessing marijuana for personal use is decriminalized in private spaces, like your hotel room, but it's still illegal. Public consumption, including visible use on balconies or in streets, is prohibited and may result in fines. Some private cannabis clubs exist, but they are members-only. So, you can keep it in your hotel room but avoid public use.

4. *Are there any regional differences in how cannabis is regulated across different areas of Spain?* **Yes.** There are regional differences in cannabis regulation in Spain. In areas like **Catalonia** and the **Basque Country**, cannabis social clubs (CSCs) are more common, and local authorities tend to be more lenient with their regulation. In contrast, **Madrid** has fewer clubs and stricter enforcement of public consumption laws. **Andalusia** is more conservative, with higher fines for public use, while in the **Balearic Islands**, there are stricter rules in tourist areas to discourage public consumption. Regulations can vary, so it's important to check local rules when traveling within Spain.

5. *What are the penalties for possessing and consuming other types of illicit drugs in Spain?* In Spain, penalties for possessing or trafficking illicit drugs like cocaine or ecstasy are severe. For **minor trafficking**, sentences range from **one to three years**, while **standard trafficking** can lead to **three to six years**. **Aggravating factors** can increase the sentence to **six to nine years**. **Possession for personal use** is usually treated as an administrative offense with fines. Hard drugs like MDMA or heroin carry harsher penalties, and repeat offenders face higher fines.

 # Law of the Land Hypothetical

HYPOTHETICAL: *Sophie, a 30-year-old digital nomad living temporarily in Madrid, joins a local cannabis social club through a friend. She receives a small amount of cannabis from the club and takes it home to use later. On her way back, she is stopped by police during a routine check and is found carrying the cannabis in her bag. Is Sophie breaking the law by transporting cannabis from a social club to her residence in Spain?*

ANSWER: ***Yes***. *Technically, Sophie is violating Spanish law. While cannabis social clubs are allowed to distribute cannabis to members for private consumption, the law requires that the cannabis be consumed on-site. Transporting it in public—even if sealed and for personal use—can be considered possession in a public space, which is illegal and can result in administrative fines. Although Sophie obtained the cannabis legally within the context of the club, carrying it outside puts her at risk of penalties.*

 # Takeaways

- Personal use and cultivation of small amounts at home are tolerated, but public possession or consumption is illegal and subject to fines.

- These clubs are allowed under strict, non-commercial conditions, but transporting cannabis outside the club can still result in legal consequences.

- Spain distinguishes between personal use and intent to distribute. While personal use results in administrative fines, trafficking leads to criminal charges and prison time.

- Travelers must carry prescriptions and doctor's notes for controlled substances. Lack of proper documentation may lead to fines or legal issues.

- Synthetic cannabinoids and other illicit substances like cocaine or ecstasy carry strict penalties, especially for trafficking, with prison sentences ranging from three to nine years.

ALCOHOL-RELATED OFFENSES

CHAPTER 5

ALCOHOL-RELATED OFFENSES

Alcohol-Related Offenses

Alcohol has long been woven into the fabric of Spanish culture, with its roots going back thousands of years to Roman and Moorish times, when wine production and viticulture began to flourish. Over the centuries, **wine** became not just a beverage, but **a symbol of hospitality, celebration, and regional identity**. In modern Spain, alcohol is not typically viewed as taboo or reserved for special occasions—rather, it is considered a normal part of everyday life, particularly when enjoyed in moderation and in the context of meals or social interaction.

Across the country, it's common to see people enjoying a glass of wine or beer with lunch or dinner, whether at home or in public. Spaniards tend to drink slowly and socially, often pairing their drinks with tapas (small plates) during gatherings with friends and family. Alcohol is also **deeply tied to regional customs and festivals**. For instance, wine plays a central role in events like the **Haro Wine Festival** in La Rioja, and beer is widely consumed during popular celebrations like **Las Fallas** in Valencia or **Feria de Abril** in Seville.

Spain is home to a variety of alcoholic beverages that reflect its diverse regions. **Red wine from Rioja and Ribera del Duero** are internationally renowned, while **cava, a sparkling wine from Catalonia**, is often served during toasts and celebrations. **Sangria**—wine mixed with fruit, juice, and sometimes spirits—is a popular choice among tourists and locals during the summer. **Sherry**, or *"jerez,"* originates from Andalusia and ranges from very dry to sweet, playing a big part in the culinary traditions of southern Spain. **Beer** (*cerveza*) is also widely consumed, with domestic brands like Mahou, Estrella Damm, Cruzcampo, and San Miguel found in nearly every bar and restaurant.

Alcohol in Spain is seen less as a means of intoxication and more as a **cultural and culinary experience.** Spaniards generally value moderation, and excessive drinking or public drunkenness is often frowned upon. While attitudes toward alcohol are relaxed compared to some other countries, laws and social expectations still guide when, where, and how alcohol is consumed, blending a deep respect for tradition with a modern approach to public safety and regulation.

Alcohol Regulation

Legally, alcohol is both accessible and regulated. The **legal drinking age in Spain is 18, and this law applies both to purchasing and consuming alcohol in public spaces.** Supermarkets and convenience stores sell alcohol throughout the day, although some regions restrict sales after a certain hour at night. Bars and restaurants typically serve alcohol until closing, and late-night venues may continue into the early morning hours. While alcohol is easy to obtain, selling or serving it to minors is illegal and can lead to fines or license revocation for businesses.

Public drinking is a more **complex issue.** In some cities and towns, especially those popular with tourists, local ordinances prohibit drinking in public spaces like streets, parks, and beaches to reduce noise, litter, and disturbances. **These anti-"*botellón*" (street drinking) laws are especially enforced during weekends and holidays, with violators subject to fines ranging from €100 to €600 or more** (approximately US$110 to $650). However, during local festivals or in smaller towns, public drinking is often more tolerated or even expected.

Alcohol regulations are enforced by local and national police, especially in nightlife areas and during festivals. Selling to minors can lead to **fines from €3,000 to €15,000** (around US$3,250 to $16,300), and businesses may face license suspension. Public intoxication isn't usually criminal, but **DUI is strictly punished**. The legal blood alcohol limit is **0.05 percent for most drivers** and **0.00 percent for new or commercial drivers**. Penalties can include **fines up to €1,000** (US$1,090), license suspension, or even jail time in serious cases.

Things to Remember

- **Drinking Age:** The legal drinking age in Spain is **18**. This applies to both purchasing and consuming alcohol in public spaces.

- **ID:** You may need to show ID to purchase alcohol, especially if you appear underage or in certain establishments.

- **Public Consumption:** Drinking alcohol in public spaces like streets, parks, or beaches is generally **restricted** in some areas, especially in tourist-heavy locations. However, it is **legal** in many smaller towns or during festivals. Local ordinances may impose fines for public drinking, particularly in areas where it's prohibited.

- **Public Drunkenness:** While public intoxication itself is not criminal, it can lead to **penalties** if it causes a disturbance or endangers public safety. Fines for public drunkenness can range from **€100 to €600** (approximately US$110 to $650), depending on the severity of the situation.

- **Drunk Driving:** The legal blood alcohol limit is **0.05 percent for regular drivers** and **0.00 percent for new or commercial drivers**. Penalties for DUI include **fines up to €1,000** (about US$1,090), **license suspension**, community service, and, in more severe cases, imprisonment (up to six months for serious offenses).

- **Purchase of Alcohol:** Alcohol can be purchased in **supermarkets, convenience stores, bars, and restaurants**. The legal sale hours are generally from **7:00AM to 10:00PM**, but some regions impose stricter rules. It's illegal to purchase alcohol **after certain hours** (especially in residential areas) and **minors cannot buy alcohol**.

- **Alcohol Permits:** For private events like parties or festivals, you generally do not need a permit unless you are **serving alcohol in public spaces** or if the event is large-scale and involves commercial transactions. Local authorities may require permits for events that involve the sale or large distribution of alcohol.

- **Illegal Alcohol:** The issue of illegal alcohol is relatively minor, but it does exist, particularly **unlicensed production** or **bootlegging** of cheap or counterfeit alcohol. The sale of illicit alcohol can result in penalties, including **fines** and **imprisonment**. There's concern over low-quality or unregulated alcohol, which could pose health risks.

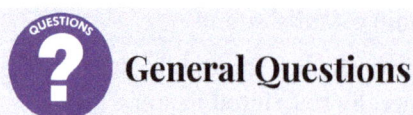 ## General Questions

1. *Can I possess an open container in public?* In Spain, **possessing an open container of alcohol in public** is generally **not allowed** in many areas, especially in tourist zones or cities with strict regulations. Public drinking laws vary by region, and many cities or municipalities have local ordinances that **prohibit open containers** in public spaces like streets, parks, and beaches. Violating these regulations can result in **fines**. However, during festivals or special events, public consumption may be permitted in certain areas with proper permits.

2. *What are the rules and regulations surrounding alcohol consumption at festivals or public events in Spain?* In Spain, alcohol consumption at festivals and public events is generally allowed, especially during major celebrations like La Tomatina or San Fermín. However, local regulations vary, with some areas restricting public drinking to maintain order. For example, street drinking may be banned in certain districts, and fines can range from **€100 to €600** (about US$110 to $650). Large events may require special permits for alcohol distribution, ensuring responsible sales and preventing underage drinking.

 **Law of the Land Hypothetical**

HYPOTHETICAL: *David, a tourist from Canada, is attending a popular music festival in Madrid. He buys a can of beer from a vendor and begins drinking it while walking around the festival grounds. A local police officer approaches him and explains that drinking alcohol in public is prohibited in that area. David is surprised because he had seen other festival-goers with drinks. Is David breaking the law by drinking alcohol in public, and what penalties could he face?*

ANSWER: ***Yes***. *David is violating local regulations. Even though festivals can sometimes allow public drinking, many areas in Spain, particularly in tourist-heavy districts, have specific local ordinances banning alcohol consumption in public spaces unless there's a permit. In this case, David may be issued a **fine**, typically ranging from €100 to €600 (about US$110 to $650), depending on the region and the enforcement of local laws. It's important for travelers to check the local rules on alcohol consumption before drinking in public areas.*

 **Takeaways**

- Alcohol is a significant part of Spanish culture and daily life. It's commonly enjoyed with meals or social gatherings, and moderate drinking is socially accepted. Excessive or disruptive drinking, however, is generally discouraged.

- The legal drinking age is **18**. While alcohol is easy to buy, drinking it in public spaces like streets or parks is often restricted in urban or tourist-heavy areas. Violations can lead to fines between €100 and €600 (US$110 to $650).

- Police actively enforce alcohol regulations, especially during festivals or in nightlife areas. Selling alcohol to minors can bring heavy fines (up to €15,000 or US$16,300), and disturbing public order due to drunkenness can also result in penalties.

- Spain enforces strict blood alcohol limits—**0.05 percent** for most drivers and **0.00 percent** for new or commercial drivers. DUI penalties can include fines up to €1,000 (US$1,090), license suspension, or even jail time for serious offenses.

- Alcohol-related laws can vary significantly between regions and cities. Some areas may be more lenient during festivals, while others have strict "no public drinking" rules. Travelers should always check local regulations to avoid unintentional offenses.

CHAPTER 6

FIREARM & AMMUNITION OFFENSES

CHAPTER 6

FIREARM & AMMUNITION OFFENSES

Current Firearm Status

In Spain, firearm ownership is tightly regulated and allowed only under very specific conditions. Citizens must be **at least 18 years old**, pass a psychological evaluation, complete firearm safety training, and pass a thorough background check that ensures they have no criminal history or ties to extremist groups. Firearms are not permitted for general self-defense purposes, which means that civilians cannot own guns simply to protect themselves. Instead, the primary legal justifications for owning a firearm are for activities like **hunting**, **sport shooting**, and **collecting**. Even in these cases, individuals must apply for and be granted **a license from the Guardia Civil** (national police), who maintain a centralized registry of all firearms and license holders in the country.

The types of firearms allowed for private ownership are also limited. **Hunting rifles** and **shotguns** are the most commonly permitted weapons, while **handguns** are far more restricted and typically **only allowed for licensed sport shooters. Semi-automatic pistols are permitted with restrictions**; for example, magazines must be below 20 rounds for some models. Different licenses are needed for shotguns versus rifles, with restrictions on calibers and firearm types. Fully automatic weapons and other military-style firearms are **prohibited entirely**. Individuals may be limited to a set number of firearms depending on the license they hold—for example, hunters may possess up to six weapons, while sport shooters with the appropriate license may own up to ten.[9]

Even if someone is licensed to own a firearm, there are **additional restrictions** on how it can be carried and used. **Civilians are not allowed to carry loaded firearms in public. Transporting a weapon is only legal if it is unloaded, locked in a case, and the person is en route to or from an authorized activity,** such as hunting or visiting a shooting range. **Using a firearm for self-defense is only legal** in extremely rare situations, such as a **direct and immediate threat where no other options are available.** In such cases, the person using the firearm would need to prove that their actions were both necessary and proportionate under Spanish law.

Misuse or illegal possession of a firearm carries serious legal consequences, including **large fines, revocation of licenses,** and **imprisonment.** Spain's strict gun laws are designed to prioritize public safety and reduce the risk of firearm-related violence, and they reflect a broader cultural approach that sees guns as tools for regulated sporting activities rather than instruments for personal protection.

Firearm Restrictions for Visitors

Generally, **tourists are prohibited from bringing firearms into the country.** However, **exceptions** exist for specific purposes like **hunting or sport shooting.**

Non-resident visitors intending to participate in hunting activities must obtain a **special permit in advance.** This process involves applying through a Spanish consulate, and requires submitting an application form, a valid passport, and other necessary documentation at least one month before travel. The firearm must be declared, and upon arrival in Spain, it is subject to inspection and must be used strictly for the

---

9   https://www.velascolawyers.com/en/civil-law/ownership-of-firearms-in-spain.html

authorized activity.[10] For visitors from EU countries, the **European Firearms Pass** (**EFP**) facilitates the temporary importation of firearms for activities like hunting or sport shooting. The EFP must be obtained in the visitor's home country and is recognized across EU member states.[11]

It's important to note that using firearms for self-defense is not a valid reason for bringing a weapon into Spain, and doing so without proper authorization can lead to severe legal consequences, including fines, confiscation of the firearm, or criminal charges. Therefore, visitors should ensure they have the appropriate permits and adhere strictly to Spanish firearm regulations.

 **Penalties**

In Spain, firearm-related offenses are governed by the Penal Code, particularly Articles 563 to 570. Penalties vary based on the nature and severity of the offense:

- **Illegal Possession:** Possessing prohibited weapons or significantly modified firearms can result in imprisonment from one to three years. Unauthorized possession of regulated firearms without the necessary licenses can lead to **six months to two years of imprisonment**, depending on the type of firearm and specific circumstances.

- **Trafficking and Smuggling:** Engaging in the unauthorized manufacture, trade, or storage of firearms or ammunition is punishable by imprisonment ranging from **six months to ten years**,

---

10 https://www.exteriores.gob.es/Consulados/sanfrancisco/en/ ServiciosConsulares/Paginas/Permit-for-hunting-guns.aspx

11 https://en.wikipedia.org/wiki/European_Firearms_Pass?utm_source

depending on the weapons involved and the individual's role in the operation.

- **Use in Crimes:** Utilizing firearms during the commission of crimes can lead to enhanced penalties, including longer prison terms and additional sanctions, reflecting the increased severity of offenses involving weapons.

- **Unauthorized Carrying:** Carrying firearms in public places without proper authorization can result in fines between €300 and €30,000 (US$337 and $337,000), confiscation of the weapon, and potential suspension or revocation of firearm licenses.

- **Organized Crime Involvement:** Participation in criminal organizations that involve the illegal possession, trafficking, or use of firearms can lead to additional penalties, including the dissolution of the organization and extended prison sentences for those involved.

 **General Questions**

1. *What happens if the police catch me carrying a firearm in Spain?* If the police catch you carrying a firearm in Spain without the proper authorization, you can face serious consequences. Depending on the situation and the type of firearm, penalties may include fines, confiscation of the weapon, loss of any existing firearm licenses, and possible criminal charges. In more severe cases, unauthorized carrying of a firearm can result in prison sentences. Spain takes unauthorized weapon possession seriously, especially in public areas.

2. *Can you bring your gun with you when traveling in Spain?*
Bringing a personal firearm into Spain is possible but highly restricted and usually limited to hunting or sport shooting. Tourists must get prior authorization from the Spanish consulate in their home country, submitting documents like a passport, hunting license (with certified Spanish translation), and firearm details. Processing can take weeks.

 ## Law of the Land True Story

In January 2023, Frank Hanebuth, the former leader of the Hells Angels in Europe, was facing trial in Spain for his role in leading a criminal empire on the island of Mallorca. From 2009 to 2013, Hanebuth oversaw a chapter of the infamous motorcycle club involved in a range of illegal activities. A critical part of their operations included the illegal possession and use of firearms, which were employed to maintain control and intimidate rivals.

Spanish prosecutors were seeking a 13-year prison sentence for Hanebuth, alongside a €4.2 million (US$4.5 million) fine.

 ## Takeaways

- In Spain, owning firearms is tightly regulated, and individuals must meet strict requirements, including passing psychological evaluations, safety training, and thorough background checks. Ownership is typically limited to hunting, sport shooting, and collecting purposes.

- Civilians cannot carry loaded firearms in public. Transporting a firearm is only allowed if it is unloaded, locked, and the person is en route to an authorized activity like hunting or visiting a shooting range.

- Tourists cannot bring firearms into Spain without proper permits, such as for hunting or sport shooting. Non-residents must apply for special permits in advance, and for EU visitors, the European Firearms Pass (EFP) is necessary for temporary firearm importation.

- Firearm offenses in Spain carry severe penalties. Illegal possession can lead to imprisonment of up to three years, while trafficking and smuggling can result in up to ten years. Unauthorized carrying of a firearm can lead to fines, confiscation, and criminal charges.

- Participation in criminal organizations involved in firearms offenses can lead to extended prison sentences and other severe penalties, including the dissolution of criminal groups involved in illegal firearm activities.

PROSTITUTION

PROSTITUTION

Overview

Prostitution in Spain exists in a legal gray area. While selling sexual services is **not criminalized**, profiting from another person's prostitution—such as **pimping or operating a brothel**—is **illegal**. In recent years, there has been increasing political debate about whether to fully legalize or abolish prostitution, with proposals emerging to criminalize both the purchase and sale of sex entirely.

The **root causes** of prostitution in Spain are largely **socio-economic**. Many individuals, particularly women from economically disadvantaged backgrounds or migrant communities, are driven into sex work by poverty, lack of employment opportunities, and the need to support families. Human trafficking is also a significant factor, with many victims coerced or deceived into prostitution by organized networks. For some, the decision to engage in sex work is voluntary but heavily influenced by financial pressure and limited social support.

Spanish society remains divided on the issue of prostitution. Some segments of the population advocate for regulation and protection of sex workers' rights, viewing it as a form of labor. Others, especially feminist groups and human rights activists, argue that prostitution is inherently exploitative and should be abolished. There is growing concern about the links between prostitution, human trafficking, and organized crime, which has led to heightened public scrutiny and ongoing political efforts to reform or redefine the legal approach to sex work in Spain.

Laws and Penalties[12]

Prostitution in Spain is **not illegal,** but it is **largely unregulated** at the national level. The sale of sex by individuals is not criminalized, but third-party involvement—such as profiting from another person's prostitution or operating brothels—is illegal under **anti-pimping laws.** Because there is no comprehensive regulatory framework, legal responses often depend on local municipal ordinances, and there is considerable variation across the country.

There are **no officially designated or legalized red-light districts** in Spain, but in practice, certain areas in cities like Barcelona or Madrid have become informal zones where street-based prostitution is more common. These areas are not officially sanctioned or protected, and regulation is left to local governments. Some municipalities have implemented ordinances to restrict or manage where and how sex work can take place, often citing concerns about public order or traffic safety.

Regulations for sex workers themselves are minimal because there is no formal recognition of prostitution as a legitimate occupation. As a result, there are **no standardized health checks, licensing systems, or labor protections** for sex workers. This legal ambiguity leaves them vulnerable to exploitation and limits access to health and legal services.

Penalties for prostitution-related infractions **generally target clients and third parties,** rather than sex workers. Individuals who organize or profit from another's prostitution, especially involving coercion or trafficking, face serious criminal charges with penalties that can include substantial fines and imprisonment. In cities with municipal bans on street prostitution, sex workers or clients may be fined, particularly if the activity is deemed to cause public nuisance. However, enforcement is inconsistent and highly localized.

---

12 https://en.wikipedia.org/wiki/Prostitution_in_Spain

Prostitution Practices

Estimates of the number of individuals involved in prostitution vary significantly. According to a 2024 study by the Ministry of Equality, approximately 114,576 women are engaged in prostitution, with about 92,496 identified as victims of trafficking. In contrast, Médicos del Mundo estimates that around 350,000 women are involved in prostitution in Spain, with 80% being undocumented migrants. The clandestine nature of the industry and the lack of official recognition contribute to the difficulty in obtaining accurate statistics.[13]

Prostitution manifests in various forms across Spain. **Street prostitution** remains visible in certain areas, while brothels, often operating under the guise of clubs or massage parlors, are prevalent despite the illegality of profiting from another's prostitution. The advent of digital technology has shifted a significant portion of the industry online, with many sex workers advertising services through websites and social media platforms, facilitating encounters in private apartments, hotels, or clients' homes.

Local authorities in Spain exhibit diverse attitudes toward prostitution, often influenced by regional policies and public sentiment. Some municipalities have implemented ordinances to regulate or restrict street prostitution, citing concerns over public order and safety. For instance, Barcelona has enacted bylaws aimed at curbing visible sex work in public spaces.

The Spanish government has been considering legislative changes to address the complexities of prostitution. In 2022, a draft law was introduced aiming to criminalize the purchase of sexual services and penalize those who financially exploit prostitutes or provide premises for prostitution. This reflects a shift toward an abolitionist model, focusing on reducing demand and combating exploitation.

---

13 https://www.lavanguardia.com/mediterranean/20240917/9947893/
woman-work-prostitution-spain-sexual-exploitation-equality-minis-
try-adult-redondo.html

Overall, prostitution in Spain remains a contentious issue, with ongoing debates surrounding legality, regulation, and the rights of sex workers. The lack of uniform policies and the clandestine nature of the industry continue to pose challenges for effective governance and the protection of those involved.

Sex Trafficking and Exploitation

Sex trafficking and exploitation are significant concerns in Spain, primarily due to its role as both a **destination and transit country for trafficking networks**. The country's large sex industry, coupled with legal ambiguity around prostitution, creates an environment where exploitation can flourish under the radar. While prostitution itself is not illegal, it is also not fully regulated, allowing traffickers to exploit legal loopholes. Organized criminal groups take advantage of this legal gray zone, often luring victims with false job promises or by using coercion and manipulation. Spain's geographic location also makes it a **strategic gateway** into Europe, particularly from Africa and Latin America, which further facilitates trafficking operations.[14]

Certain parts of Spain are more vulnerable to trafficking than others. Major cities like **Madrid, Barcelona**, and **Valencia** are **prominent hotspots** due to their large populations, tourism, and thriving nightlife scenes, which generate high demand for sexual services.[15] **Coastal regions** with high tourist traffic, such as the **Costa del Sol**, also experience heightened activity. **Border cities and port areas**—such as **Algeciras**, and the Spanish enclaves of **Ceuta** and **Melilla** in North Africa—are key entry points for trafficked individuals. Additionally, **rural agricultural areas** in the south, such as **Almería** and **Murcia**, are known for labor

---

14   https://www.vaia.com/en-us/explanations/spanish/spanish-social-issues/human-trafficking-spain/

15   https://www.statista.com/statistics/1300857/number-victims-sex-trafficking-spain-by-region/

exploitation that sometimes overlaps with sexual exploitation, especially among migrant populations.[16]

The demographics most at risk include **migrant women and girls**, especially from Latin America (such as Colombia and Brazil), Eastern Europe (notably Romania and Bulgaria), Sub-Saharan Africa (with a high number from Nigeria), and Asia. These individuals are often undocumented or have precarious legal status, making them more susceptible to coercion and less likely to seek help due to fear of deportation or retaliation. **Minors in the child welfare system and LGBTQ+ youth,** particularly transgender individuals, are also highly vulnerable due to marginalization, lack of support, and increased exposure to exploitation.

The Spanish government has taken several steps to combat sex trafficking, though challenges remain. It has implemented the **National Strategy against Human Trafficking for the Purpose of Sexual and Labor Exploitation** (2021–2023), which focuses on prevention, victim protection, and prosecution.[17] Specialized police units, like **UCRIF,** target human trafficking networks, and Spain collaborates with non-governmental organizations to offer victim support services such as legal aid, shelters, and psychological assistance. Awareness campaigns aim to educate both the public and vulnerable communities. Nevertheless, critics argue that more proactive victim identification is needed and that protections often depend on victims' cooperation with law enforcement. The lack of comprehensive prostitution regulation also continues to complicate efforts to clearly distinguish between voluntary sex work and exploitation.[18]

---

16 https://www.theolivepress.es/spain-news/2023/03/21/
    nine-brothels-dismantled-and-16-women-freed-in-various-towns-across-s

17 https://eucpn.org/document/spain-national-strategic-plan-against-hu-
    man-trafficking-and-labour-exploitation-2021-2023

18 https://www.spainenglish.com/2025/02/24/spanish-police-smash-sex-
    trafficking-gang-that-exploited-more-than-1000-women/

 ## Sex Tourism and Public Health

Sex tourism is present in Spain, although it operates in a somewhat discreet and informal manner compared to other countries where it may be more openly promoted. Spain's permissive stance on prostitution—where the exchange of sex for money is legal—has contributed to the development of a **commercial sex industry** that can attract both local and foreign tourists seeking sexual services. The country's popularity as a tourist destination, its nightlife culture, and the presence of legal gray areas around sex work make it an appealing location for sex tourism.

Popular sex tourism destinations in Spain include major cities such as **Barcelona, Madrid,** and **Valencia**, where there is both a high demand and a well-developed nightlife. Additionally, **tourist-heavy coastal areas** like the **Costa del Sol**, particularly **Marbella** and **Benidorm**, as well as **Ibiza** and parts of the **Canary Islands**, have reputations for vibrant party scenes that may include commercial sex offerings. These locations are frequented by both domestic and international tourists, some of whom are drawn by the availability of sexual services in clubs, private apartments, and escort services.

Sex tourism in Spain is typically organized and advertised through a mix of **online platforms, escort websites, adult classifieds,** and **social media.** Many establishments operate under the guise of "clubs" or "massage parlors," and there are even travel websites or forums where tourists share experiences and reviews of sex services. While not formally advertised in mainstream tourism campaigns, the accessibility of sex services is often known through word of mouth or specific online communities.

Public health concerns associated with sex tourism in Spain are significant. The primary concerns include the **spread of sexually transmitted infections (STIs)** such as HIV, gonorrhea, and syphilis, particularly in cases where condom use is inconsistent or discouraged. Vulnerable populations, including trafficked individuals and undocumented migrant sex workers, often lack access to regular medical care and may be hesitant to seek help due to fear of legal consequences or deportation. Furthermore, the informal nature of much of the sex work industry makes health outreach and regulation challenging. This is compounded by issues like mental health stress, substance abuse, and gender-based violence among individuals involved in the sex industry—especially those who are coerced or trafficked.

Spain's public health authorities and non-government organizations attempt to mitigate these concerns through **harm reduction programs**, **mobile health clinics**, and **awareness campaigns** focused on safe sex and STI prevention. However, the legal ambiguity of prostitution and the hidden nature of many sex tourism activities make consistent regulation and health monitoring difficult.

Tips to Avoid Being Solicited

- Areas like *El Raval* in Barcelona, parts of *Gran Vía* in Madrid, and nightlife strips in places like *Marbella* or *Benidorm* are known for sex work visibility. Staying in well-lit, central, and family-oriented zones can reduce encounters.

- In nightlife areas, sex workers or promoters might directly approach tourists. Politely but firmly say *"No, gracias,"* and keep walking. Avoid prolonged eye contact or stopping to chat, as that can be taken as interest.

- Some clubs, bars, or massage parlors double as fronts for sex work. If a venue seems vague about its services or has a "members only" or "private shows" policy, it may be best to skip it. Research places beforehand through Google Maps reviews or local guides.

- Searching for nightlife or entertainment on generic or adult-friendly websites can lead to pop-ups or links that promote escort services. Stick to verified travel and event websites to avoid being funneled into adult content.

- Flashy outfits, public drunkenness, or wandering solo in the early hours can make someone appear like an easy target. Blending in with locals and moving confidently with a group can discourage unwanted attention.

 ## Law of the Land True Story[19]

In March 2023, Spanish authorities uncovered a major sex trafficking operation, dismantling nine brothels across Barcelona, Alicante, Mallorca, and Girona, and rescuing 16 Chinese women who had been trafficked and forced into prostitution. The victims were subjected to physical abuse and confined in unsanitary, cramped living conditions, all under the control of an organized crime group. The operation led to multiple arrests and exposed the alarming reality of exploitation hidden within Spain's urban centers.

This case reflects key themes from our chapter on human trafficking, especially the vulnerability of migrant populations and the covert nature of trafficking networks that stretch across regions. The fact that these crimes occurred in multiple municipalities underscores the complexity and reach of trafficking, making inter-agency cooperation essential.

The incident also raises important public health and human rights concerns. The women have since been offered social support services, highlighting the need for trauma recovery programs and protective measures. Spain's approach—combining law enforcement with victim-centered care—aligns with broader European efforts to combat human trafficking through prevention, prosecution, and support.

---

19 https://www.theolivepress.es/spain-news/2023/03/21/
nine-brothels-dismantled-and-16-women-freed-in-various-towns-across-s

Takeaways

- While prostitution isn't illegal, profiting from it is. This legal gray area allows traffickers to operate with little oversight.

- Cities like Barcelona have crackdowns, but others don't, creating uneven enforcement and protection across the country.

- Undocumented women from Latin America, Africa, Eastern Europe, and Asia are most vulnerable due to coercion and fear of deportation.

- Spain's location and tourism make it a key hub for trafficking, especially in cities like Madrid, Barcelona, and coastal regions.

- Efforts like the National Strategy and specialized police units help, but protection often hinges on victim cooperation, and legal ambiguity persists.

LGBTQ

- Homophobia in Spain
- LGBTQ Legislation
- LGBTQ Tourism and Safety Concerns
- General Questions
- Law of the Land Hypothetical

LGBTQ

Homophobia in Spain

Spain has made significant strides in LGBTQ+ rights, although challenges persist. Historically, under Francisco Franco's dictatorship from 1939 to 1975, homosexuality was criminalized, and LGBTQ+ individuals were imprisoned, surveilled, or institutionalized. After Franco's death, Spain transitioned toward democracy and began dismantling these repressive policies. By 2005, **Spain became the third country in the world to legalize same-sex marriage**, marking a dramatic shift in public policy and social values.[20]

Today, Spain is widely regarded as **one of the most LGBTQ+-friendly countries in Europe**. Major cities like Madrid and Barcelona celebrate Pride with massive, inclusive events, and even small towns such as Campillo de Ranas have become symbolic centers for same-sex weddings. That said, acceptance can vary by region, with some rural or conservative areas maintaining more traditional views.

Although Catholicism remains culturally significant in Spain, the Church's influence on law and politics has declined, allowing for more progressive developments in LGBTQ+ rights. However, certain religious or socially conservative groups continue to push back against this progress, contributing to lingering prejudice and discriminatory rhetoric. In

---

20 https://en.wikipedia.org/wiki/Same-sex_marriage_in_Spain

daily life, homophobia may appear in subtle forms such as **workplace bias, bullying in schools**, or **rejection by family members**. A 2024 EU report revealed that 53 percent of LGBTQ+ people in Spain reported experiencing harassment over the past year, suggesting that stigma remains a real concern even in progressive environments.[21]

Violence and overt discrimination also persist. In 2022, there were 189 officially recorded hate crimes related to sexual orientation or gender identity in Spain.[22] One particularly high-profile case was the 2021 murder of Samuel Luiz, a young gay man whose death led to widespread protests and the eventual conviction of four people for his killing (see *Law of the Land True Story* below).

Public figures have played a role in advancing LGBTQ+ visibility and rights. Singer **Miguel Garena** has spoken out against homophobic attacks, and the popular TV series *Veneno* spotlighted the life of transgender icon **Cristina Ortiz**, helping bring trans issues into mainstream Spanish media.

Despite its reputation for progressiveness, Spain continues to grapple with the social and structural barriers that impact LGBTQ+ individuals, particularly in more conservative regions. Continued advocacy, education, and policy development are essential to ensure full inclusion and protection for all.

LGBTQ Legislation

Spain is widely recognized as **one of the most LGBTQ+-friendly countries in Europe**. Homosexuality was **decriminalized in 1979**, following the end of the Franco dictatorship, and **in 2005, Spain became the third country in the world to legalize same-sex marriage**, also

---

21 https://www.surinenglish.com/six/report-finds-that-lgtbi-spaniards-have-suffered-20240517095256-nt.html

22 https://www.statista.com/statistics/1454327/reports-of-anti-lgbt-hate-crimes/

granting same-sex couples the right to adopt children. These laws reflect a broader framework that is supportive of LGBTQ+ rights.

Spanish legislation includes several measures aimed at protecting LGBTQ+ individuals. There are legal protections against discrimination based on sexual orientation and gender identity in areas such as employment, education, and access to goods and services. The country's anti-discrimination framework is reinforced by both national laws and regional statutes, some of which are even more progressive. **In 2023, Spain passed a landmark gender recognition law that allows individuals over 16 to change their legal gender without medical or psychological certification**. This law also bans conversion therapy nationwide.[23]

While national laws are generally inclusive, support for LGBTQ+ rights can vary by region. **Urban areas** such as Madrid, Barcelona, and Valencia tend to be **more progressive** and have more visible LGBTQ+ communities, events, and services. These cities often host large Pride celebrations and have municipal anti-discrimination ordinances. Conversely, **rural or traditionally conservative regions**—particularly parts of Castilla-La Mancha or Extremadura—can be **less visibly supportive**, and LGBTQ+ individuals there may experience more social stigma or lack of local protections.

LGBTQ Tourism and Safety Concerns

LGBTQ+ tourism is highly developed in Spain, with the country being one of the most LGBTQ+-friendly destinations in the world. Major cities and coastal areas actively promote inclusive tourism, and many regions have vibrant queer communities, events, and nightlife that attract visitors globally. Spain is home to some of Europe's largest and most popular LGBTQ+ events, including **Madrid Pride**, one of the biggest in Europe, and **Barcelona Pride**, known for its beach parties and cultural events. The town of **Sitges**, near Barcelona, has a large gay scene and is a

---

23 https://www.lgbtqnation.com/2023/02/
    spain-passes-landmark-gender-recognition-law/

hotspot for international LGBTQ+ tourists, while **Gran Canaria**, particularly the area of Maspalomas, is famous for its year-round gay-friendly atmosphere and events like **Winter Pride** and the **Maspalomas Gay Carnival.**

Public displays of affection, such as holding hands or kissing, are generally acceptable and safe in major cities and LGBTQ+-friendly towns in Spain. The country's progressive laws and open culture mean that same-sex couples can usually express affection without issue, particularly in cosmopolitan areas. However, levels of tolerance can vary by region. **More tolerant areas** include **Madrid, Barcelona, Sitges, Valencia, Ibiza,** and **Gran Canaria**, all widely recognized for their openness and inclusivity. In contrast, **rural regions and conservative provinces**, especially in **central or southern Spain,** may exhibit more traditional or religious values, which can lead to occasional discomfort or stares for LGBTQ+ individuals.

In terms of safety, **Spain is considered a safe destination for LGBTQ+ travelers, with relatively low rates of violence** compared to many other countries. However, **isolated incidents of verbal harassment** or **rare physical attacks** can still occur, particularly late at night or outside popular clubs. As with any destination, it is advisable to stay aware of one's surroundings and use common sense, especially in unfamiliar or conservative settings. Overall, LGBTQ+ visitors will find Spain a welcoming, open, and safe place to travel.

 **General Questions**

1. ***Do laws in Spain protect homosexual expressions and conduct?* Yes.** Laws in Spain protect homosexual expressions and conduct. Homosexuality has been legal in Spain since 1979, and same-sex couples have been able to marry legally since 2005, under the **Spanish Marriage Equality Law**. This law grants same-sex couples the same legal rights and protections as heterosexual couples, including inheritance, taxation, and social security benefits. Additionally, Spain has legal protections against discrimination based on sexual orientation in various areas, including employment, education, and public services. The country also passed a Gender Identity Law, which allows individuals to change their gender legally without requiring surgery.

2. ***How widely accepted are same-sex couples in public spaces such as hotels, restaurants, and tourist attractions across different regions of Spain?*** Same-sex couples are widely accepted in public spaces across most of Spain, especially in cities like Madrid, Barcelona, Valencia, and tourist hotspots like Sitges and Ibiza, where LGBTQ+ culture is vibrant and integrated. Hotels, restaurants, and attractions in these areas are typically welcoming, and public displays of affection are generally unproblematic.

   However, in smaller towns or more conservative rural regions, traditional values may still influence attitudes. While overt hostility is rare, subtle discomfort can occur.

 **Law of the Land Hypothetical**

HYPOTHETICAL: *Mark and Lucas, a married same-sex couple from England, are traveling through Spain on vacation. While staying in a rural village in southern Spain, they are refused service at a small*

family-run bed and breakfast after mentioning they are a married couple. The owner says she doesn't "support that lifestyle" and asks them to leave. Is it legal in Spain for a business to refuse service to someone based on their sexual orientation?

ANSWER: *No. Spain prohibits discrimination based on sexual orientation under both national and regional laws. The Spanish Constitution guarantees equality and non-discrimination, and specific laws—such as the Law for the Effective Equality of LGBTI People passed in 2023— explicitly outlaw discrimination in access to goods and services, including accommodations.*

Mark and Lucas would have the right to file a complaint with local authorities or Spain's Equality Council. Depending on the region, the business could face fines or sanctions. Spain takes LGBTQ+ rights seriously, and even in more conservative areas, such behavior can be legally challenged.

 ## Law of the Land True Story[24]

Samuel Luiz, a 24-year-old nursing assistant, was brutally attacked on July 3, 2021, outside a nightclub in A Coruña, Spain. While on a video call, passersby mistakenly thought he was filming them. One of the attackers shouted homophobic slurs and began punching Luiz. The initial assault escalated when about a dozen people chased him over roughly 250 meters, beating him for around 15 minutes until he fell unconscious. Despite one witness trying to intervene, the attackers continued until he succumbed to severe head trauma and died in hospital the next day.

His death sparked massive protests across Spain under banners like "Justice for Samuel" and "Your homophobia is killing us," with demonstrations in major cities including Madrid and Barcelona.

---

24 https://english.elpais.com/society/2021-07-12/murder-of-samuel-luiz-galvanizes-spains-lgbtq-community-there-is-no-going-back.html

In November 2024, a jury convicted three men for aggravated murder, finding that Montaña acted with homophobic intent, while a fourth man was found guilty as an accomplice. Sentences ranged from 10 to 24 years, and the court awarded over €303,000 in compensation to the victim's family. This case became a landmark moment in Spain's fight against anti-LGBTQ+ hate crimes and prompted broader societal reflection on homophobia.

SEXUALLY MOTIVATED/ VIOLENT CRIMES

CHAPTER 9
SEXUALLY MOTIVATED/ VIOLENT CRIMES

Overview

Sexually motivated crimes **remain a significant concern** in Spain, despite recent declines in convictions. In 2023, convictions for sexual offenses decreased by 10.4 percent among adults (2,867 cases) and by 15.4 percent among minors (424 cases), marking the first drop since 2017. Nonetheless, underreporting persists; a 2023 survey revealed that nearly 22 percent of women in Spain have experienced some form of sexual assault, equating to approximately 3.5 million individuals.[25]

Women, particularly those aged 15 to 44, are disproportionately affected. In 2023, the Catalan Health System identified 10,805 cases of gender-based violence, with 67.6 percent involving women in this age group. Additionally, 88 percent of the 624 individuals treated for sexual violence at Barcelona's Clínic Hospital between January and October 2024 were women.[26]

25 https://cadenaser.com/nacional/2024/09/24/bajan-las-condenas-por-delitos-sexuales-un-104-en-los-adultos-y-un-154-en-menores-cadena-ser

26 https://www.catalannews.com/society-science/item/catalan-police-receive-1910-reports-of-sexual-assault-in-first-six-months-of-year

Regional disparities are notable. In 2023, Catalonia reported over 4,000 cases of sexual violence, while Andalusia had more than 3,400. Conversely, the autonomous city of Ceuta registered only 42 cases. The Balearic Islands, including Palma, exhibited high rates of gender-based violence, with a 35 percent increase in protection orders in 2023 compared to the previous year.[27]

Contributing factors to sexually motivated crimes in Spain include persistent societal attitudes that downplay sexual violence. A 2023 poll indicated that 74 percent of respondents believe women often refrain from reporting assaults, and 9 percent felt that non-consensual touching should not be considered an offense. High-profile cases, such as the 2016 "La Manada" gang rape during Pamplona's San Fermín festival, have spurred national debates and led to legal reforms emphasizing consent.[28]

In response, Spain has implemented progressive legislation, including the "only yes means yes" law, which centers consent in sexual assault cases. However, challenges remain in addressing underreporting and ensuring consistent application of laws across regions.[29]

Related Legislation

Spain has enacted comprehensive legislation to address sexually motivated crimes, focusing on both prevention and the protection of victims. One of the most significant legal reforms is the 2022 "Ley de Garantía Integral de la Libertad Sexual" (commonly known as the "only yes means yes" law), which redefined sexual violence in legal terms. This law eliminates the distinction between "abuse" and "assault," recognizing

---

27 https://www.statista.com/statistics/1488382/number-of-sexual-vio-lence-reported-to-the-authorities-spain-region/?utm_source

28 https://www.theolivepress.es/spain-news/2023/02/08/poll-22-of-women-in-spain-say-they-have-been-sexually-assaulted

29 https://www.theguardian.com/world/2022/aug/25/spain-only-yes-means-yes-sexual-consent-bill-expected-to-become-law

any sexual act without explicit consent as assault, thereby simplifying prosecution and centering the concept of **affirmative consent**.

Penalties for sexual offenses under the revised law include **prison sentences ranging from 1 to 15 years**, depending on the severity and circumstances (such as use of violence, involvement of minors, or group assaults). The law also allows for **restraining orders**, **removal from the family home**, and **GPS monitoring** of offenders.

Enforcement has been strengthened through the creation of **specialized courts and training for judges and police**, aiming to improve the treatment of survivors and increase conviction rates. Victim protections include **free legal counsel**, **psychological support**, and **emergency housing**, and victims are no longer required to file formal complaints to receive assistance.

However, enforcement consistency varies by region. While urban areas like **Madrid, Barcelona**, and **Valencia** benefit from more robust resources and victim services, **rural areas often face slower judicial processes and limited access to specialized support**. Nonetheless, Spain remains at the forefront of progressive legal responses to sexual violence in Europe, continuing to adapt its legal framework to prioritize survivor rights and accountability.

General Questions

1. ***Do laws in Spain related to sex crimes protect the victims equally?* Yes.** Spain's sex crime laws aim to protect all victims equally, especially under the 2022 "Only Yes Means Yes" law, which emphasizes affirmative consent and provides support services even without a formal complaint. The law removes distinctions between sexual abuse and assault, strengthening protections across the board. However, in practice, certain groups—such as undocumented migrants, LGBTQ+ individuals, and sex workers—often face additional challenges in reporting crimes or accessing justice. Regional differences in enforcement and resources can also impact the consistency of protection.

2. ***Pursuant to law, what is the age of consent for sex in Spain?*** The age of consent for sex in Spain is **16 years old**, as established by law in 2015. This applies regardless of gender or sexual orientation. However, there are close-in-age exemptions to avoid criminalizing consensual relationships between teenagers close in age.

Law of the Land Hypothetical

HYPOTHETICAL: *Martina attends a house party in Seville, where she meets Javier. They drink and dance, and Javier takes a photo of her while she's clearly intoxicated. Later, Martina sees the photo posted on Javier's Instagram story without her consent. He also shares a suggestive video of her dancing in a WhatsApp group with sexual comments. Martina feels violated and reports him to the police. Can Javier be held criminally liable for sharing sexually suggestive images of Martina without her consent, even if she's not nude?*

ANSWER: *Yes. Under Spanish law, especially the "Only Yes Means Yes" law and data protection statutes, non-consensual sharing of intimate or sexually suggestive content can be criminal—even if the person is clothed. When done to harass, objectify, or humiliate, it may constitute digital sexual violence or violation of privacy, punishable by fines, prison, or restraining orders.*

 **Takeaways**

- The 2022 "Only Yes Means Yes" law centers on affirmative consent, treating any non-consensual sexual act as sexual assault, which simplifies prosecution and strengthens victim protections.

- Despite a decline in convictions, underreporting of sexual violence is high, with surveys indicating that 22 percent of women in Spain have experienced sexual assault, highlighting a gap between actual incidents and official cases.

- This age group is disproportionately impacted by sexual violence, as shown by data from regions like Catalonia and hospitals in Barcelona, where most victims are women in this demographic.

- Urban areas such as Madrid and Barcelona offer better victim services and judicial processes, while rural areas face slower justice and fewer resources, leading to unequal protection across regions.

- A significant portion of the population still holds victim-blaming attitudes, with many believing women don't report assaults or that non-consensual touching isn't a crime. High-profile cases have sparked important national debates, influencing legal reforms.

ARRESTED IN SPAIN

CHAPTER 10
ARRESTED IN SPAIN

Overview

When traveling in a foreign country, it's imperative to recognize that you are subject to the legal jurisdiction and regulations of that nation. These laws may significantly differ from those in your home country and might not offer the same legal protections you are accustomed to. It's crucial to bear in mind that penalties for violating foreign laws can be more severe than those for similar offenses in your home country, and ignorance of these laws is not typically accepted as a defense.

The consequences of breaking the law while abroad can be severe and may include expulsion, fines, arrest, or imprisonment. Even unintentional violations can lead to serious legal repercussions. It is essential for travelers to be aware of and adhere to the laws of the host country to avoid legal entanglements and ensure a safe and enjoyable experience.

Specifically, stringent penalties are often enforced for possession, use, or trafficking of illegal drugs in many countries. Convicted offenders can expect severe consequences, including lengthy jail sentences and hefty fines. The legal processes for foreigners in the event of an arrest abroad involve being charged or indicted, prosecuted, potentially convicted and sentenced, and, if applicable, going through an appeals process.

Navigating a foreign legal system can be complex, and individuals arrested abroad must be prepared to comply with the legal procedures of the host country. Seeking legal representation and understanding the local legal nuances are crucial steps for those facing legal issues in a foreign jurisdiction.

Awareness of and adherence to the laws of a foreign country are paramount when traveling. Understanding the potential consequences for legal violations and being prepared to navigate the legal system of the host country are essential aspects of responsible international travel.

Arrest Process

In Spain, the criminal justice system involves a range of common charges, which vary from minor offenses to more serious crimes. Common criminal charges include theft, which can involve taking someone else's property with or without force; assault, which refers to causing physical harm or threatening harm to another person; sexual offenses, including sexual assault, harassment, or exploitation; drug-related crimes, such as the possession, trafficking, or production of illegal substances; public disorder offenses, which can include disturbing the peace, vandalism, or public intoxication; and domestic violence, referring to abuse or violence within intimate relationships.

The **arrest process** in Spain begins when the police have reasonable suspicion or witness testimony to detain someone. For more serious crimes, the police may need a **warrant issued by a judge**, although they can arrest someone without one in urgent situations. Upon arrest, individuals are informed of their rights, similar to the Miranda Rights in the U.S., which include the right to remain silent, the right to legal representation (with free legal aid if necessary), and the right to be informed of the charges they face. During interrogation, the person has the option to remain silent and is entitled to have a lawyer present.

After the arrest, a suspect can be held in detention for **up to 72 hours** without being charged while the investigation continues. They will then appear before a judge, who will review the case. The judge can decide to release the individual on bail or order continued detention if the crime is serious. If charges are pressed, a prosecutor will determine whether to proceed with formal charges or dismiss the case. If charges are filed, the case will go to trial, with serious offenses being handled by a criminal court.

For **foreigners**, there are some special considerations. If the individual does not speak Spanish, they have **the right to an interpreter** to ensure they understand the charges and proceedings. Foreign nationals are also entitled to contact their embassy or consulate, which can offer legal support and ensure the individual's fair treatment. Additionally, foreigners who cannot afford a lawyer are eligible for **free legal aid**, just like Spanish citizens. If the individual is detained and is in the country illegally, they may be held in specialized detention centers, and there could be additional legal implications, such as deportation after serving any sentence if convicted of a serious crime.

Rights of the Arrested Person

In Spain, anyone who is arrested—whether a Spanish citizen or a foreigner—has several important legal protections. First, the police must inform the person of the **reason for their arrest** and their rights immediately, and this has to be done in a language the person understands. They have the **right to remain silent**, which means they don't have to answer any questions or make a statement.

They also have the **right to legal representation**. If they don't have their own lawyer, the state will provide one for free. The lawyer can be present during all police or court interrogations. The arrested person also has the **right to inform a relative or another person about their detention**. If the person is a foreigner, they also have the **right to contact their country's consulate or embassy**.

Another protection is the **right to a medical exam**—this can be requested or provided automatically depending on the situation. Importantly, **no one can be held by the police for more than 72 hours without seeing a judge**. After that point, the judge decides whether to release them, keep them in custody, or take other legal steps.

For foreigners, a few additional guarantees apply. They have the **right to a free interpreter** if they don't speak Spanish, and all key documents must be translated for them. Their consulate can assist with legal or practical issues, including visiting them in custody. Being arrested could also have immigration consequences, such as affecting a residency permit, but they **can't be deported without a fair legal process.**

Getting Legal Assistance

To get qualified legal assistance in Spain, you have a few reliable options whether you are a resident, visitor, or foreign national. If you can afford **private representation**, you can hire a lawyer directly. Most cities have local **Bar Associations**—like **ICAM** in Madrid[30] or **ICAB** in Barcelona[31]—where you can search for qualified lawyers by specialty or language. There are also expat-friendly directories like **Just Landed**[32] and **Expatica**[33] that list English-speaking legal professionals.

If you cannot afford a lawyer, you are entitled to free legal assistance under Spain's **legal aid system** (*abogado de oficio*). This applies to both citizens and foreigners, provided you meet certain income thresholds. If you are arrested, you can request this assistance immediately from the police. They are legally required to inform you of this right and provide access to a court-appointed lawyer at no cost. This also applies if you don't speak Spanish—an interpreter must be provided for free. You can also apply for legal aid outside of detention by contacting the Bar Association in your area.

---

30 https://www.icam.es/

31 https://www.icab.cat/

32 https://www.justlanded.com/english/Spain/Spain-Guide/Money/Lawyers-in-Spain

33 https://www.expatica.com/es/legal/

 For more information on this process, please visit the official portal of the **General Council of Spanish Lawyers** at **https://www.abogacia.es/servicios/ciudadanos/ asistencia-juridica-gratuita/**.

Foreign nationals should also reach out to their **embassy or consulate** for help. While embassies cannot provide legal representation or interfere in court cases, they can give you a list of trusted local lawyers and help ensure that your rights are respected.

If you are arrested or detained, it's essential to say clearly, "*Quiero un abogado*" ("I want a lawyer"). You do not have to answer any questions until your lawyer is present. If you don't have a lawyer, one will be provided to you for free at this early stage regardless of your financial situation, as protected by Spanish law and international rights standards.

Bail

Spain does have a bail system, but it functions differently than in some other countries like the United States. **Bail** (*fianza*) is used to guarantee that a person accused of a crime will comply with judicial proceedings and appear in court. **It is not automatic and is determined by a judge during the initial court hearing, which must occur within 72 hours of arrest.**[34]

The judge can choose to release the accused without conditions, impose bail, or order preventive detention. Bail may be **financial**—requiring a deposit with the court—or **non-financial**, involving conditions like surrendering a passport or reporting periodically to authorities. The amount of financial bail is set based on the seriousness of the crime, the accused's financial situation, risk of fleeing, and potential interference with evidence or witnesses.

---

34 https://gestiomaresme.cat/en/ rights-of-detainees-in-spain-a-complete-legal-guide/

For foreign nationals and tourists, bail decisions are often stricter due to the perceived higher flight risk. Judges may impose higher bail amounts or deny bail entirely if the person lacks strong ties to Spain, such as permanent residence, family, or employment. Courts may also require foreign defendants to surrender travel documents and remain in the country until their case is resolved.[35]

Unlike in some countries, commercial bail bondsmen do not operate in Spain. **Bail must be paid directly to the court, usually via bank transfer or certified deposit.** Embassies and consulates may assist their nationals by offering legal information or lists of local lawyers, but they cannot post bail or intervene in legal decisions.

Complaints Against Police

In Spain, the general reputation of the police is **mixed** and **can vary by region and the specific branch involved.** The **Policía Nacional** and the **Guardia Civil** are the two main national police forces, while cities and municipalities also maintain their own **Policía Local.** In major cities and tourist areas, the police are generally regarded as professional and competent. However, concerns have been raised by citizens and rights organizations about certain practices, particularly regarding the use of force and treatment of minorities. These concerns have been highlighted by international watchdogs such as Amnesty International and Human Rights Watch, which have reported instances of excessive force, racial profiling, and lack of accountability within the system.

The most common complaints against the police in Spain include the **excessive use of force** during protests or arrests, **racial or ethnic discrimination** especially targeting Roma individuals, North Africans, and Black residents, **verbal abuse or intimidation during encounters**, and **delays or lack of transparency in investigations of police misconduct.** Such incidents are most frequently reported during large-scale demonstrations, immigration controls, and, in some cases, involving vulnerable individuals in custody.

---

35 https://www.fairtrials.org/app/uploads/2022/01/Spain-advice-note.pdf

How to File a Complaint Against the Police

If you wish to **file a complaint against the police** in Spain, there are a few pathways available. You can file a complaint **directly at a police station** by stating that you want to *"presentar una denuncia"* against an officer. It's strongly advised to bring a Spanish speaker or lawyer to assist with the process. Alternatively, you can **submit your complaint to the Defensor del Pueblo**, Spain's independent national ombudsman. This office investigates grievances against public institutions, including police forces. Complaints can be filed online through their official site at **https://www.defensordelpueblo.es/en/**.

For more serious accusations such as physical abuse or misconduct involving rights violations, a legal complaint can be filed **through the courts.**

Several human rights organizations in Spain can also help. **Amnesty International Spain**[36] and **Rights International Spain**[37] both provide support and advocacy for victims of police abuse. The **Defensor del Pueblo** can be reached toll-free from within Spain at +34 900 101 025.

If you are a foreigner, your country's embassy or consulate can also assist you in navigating the complaint process or connecting you with legal resources. Documenting the incident thoroughly and seeking legal advice is highly recommended in these cases.

---

36 https://www.es.amnesty.org
     email: informacion@es.amnesty.org
     phone: +34 913 104 366

37 https://www.rightsinternationalspain.org
     email: info@rightsinternationalspain.org

General Questions

1. ***If I am convicted in Spain, am I likely to be released on bail pending the outcome of my appeal?*** In Spain, if you are convicted and want to appeal, bail pending appeal is not automatically granted and depends on several factors. The court will consider the severity of your crime, whether you pose a flight risk, and whether you have strong ties to Spain. For less severe crimes, especially those with a prison sentence of less than two years, bail is more likely, particularly if there's a reasonable chance your appeal will succeed. However, for serious offenses or foreign nationals, bail may be denied due to the risk of fleeing.

    Foreigners may be required to surrender their passport or follow additional conditions to stay in Spain for the appeal. It's best to consult with a lawyer to evaluate the chances of bail in your case.

2. ***If I am arrested, how soon will I see a judge or magistrate?*** In Spain, if you are arrested, you are required to see a judge or magistrate within **72 hours** of your detention. This is in line with Spanish law, which mandates that individuals be brought before a judge promptly to determine whether they should be released, granted bail, or kept in detention. During this initial appearance, the judge will review the circumstances of your arrest and decide on the next steps, including whether charges should be pressed, if bail should be granted, or if preventive detention is necessary.

3. ***Will I be able to contact my country's embassy in Spain?*** **Yes.** If you are arrested in Spain, you have the right to contact your country's embassy or consulate. Spanish law ensures that foreign nationals detained or arrested can contact their embassy, though this right is not automatically provided to you by the police. You must request it yourself. The police must allow you to make this communication, though it may not be immediate, especially if you are in the middle of questioning or detention.

JAILS VS. PRISONS: CONDITIONS & CULTURE

JAILS VS. PRISONS: CONDITIONS & CULTURE

Overview

Spain's prison system is structured to balance security with rehabilitation, operating under the **Ministry of the Interior's General Secretariat of Penitentiary Institutions.** The system comprises various facility types, including closed, semi-open, and open prisons, each designed to accommodate inmates based on the severity of their offenses and rehabilitation needs.

The Spanish prison system is governed by the 1979 Penitentiary Organic Law, emphasizing re-education and social rehabilitation. This legal framework has undergone reforms to align with European human rights standards, focusing on reducing overcrowding and enhancing inmate welfare.[38]

In Spain, **the term "jail" is not commonly used**; instead, facilities are categorized based on **security levels. Closed prisons** are for individuals convicted of serious crimes, offering limited freedom. **Semi-open prisons** allow inmates more freedom, such as work release programs,

---

38 onobservatory.org/upload/PrisonconditionsinSpain.pdf

and **open prisons** provide the most freedom, supporting reintegration efforts.[39]

Prisons in Spain operate under the Ministry of the Interior, with oversight from the General Secretariat of Penitentiary Institutions. Each facility is managed by a director and staff trained in correctional services. The system emphasizes rehabilitation through education, vocational training, and psychological support. Inmates are assessed to determine appropriate security levels and rehabilitation programs.

Despite reforms, Spain's prison system faces challenges such as **overcrowding**, especially in closed facilities. The transition from punitive measures to rehabilitation-focused approaches requires ongoing investment and adaptation. Additionally, ensuring adequate mental health care and addressing the needs of diverse inmate populations remain priorities.

Spain offers a range of **rehabilitation programs**, including basic and higher education, vocational training, psychological counseling, and work release opportunities. The open prison model has been particularly effective, with studies indicating lower recidivism rates among inmates who progress through this system. These programs aim to equip inmates with skills and support for successful reintegration into society.

Prison Conditions and Living Environment

In Spain, the three main types of prison facilities—**closed, semi-open, and open prisons**—offer different living conditions, depending on the level of security and freedom permitted.

Closed prisons have the **most restrictive conditions**. These are high-security institutions where inmates spend a significant portion of the day in their cells, often under close supervision. Movement within the facility is limited, and access to work, education, or recreational activities is

---

39 https://www.thetimes.com/uk/politics/article/send-convicts-to-open-prisons-to-ease-crowding-says-sentencing-tsar-5d267zd9k

more controlled. These prisons tend to be more crowded, and the environment can be tense due to the nature of the offenses and the overall structure of confinement.

Semi-open prisons offer **more leniency**. Inmates may be allowed to leave the facility during the day to work, attend school, or participate in rehabilitation programs but must return by evening. Inside the prison, conditions are somewhat less restrictive. Inmates usually have greater access to communal areas and programs, and the overall environment is less rigid than in closed institutions. These prisons serve as transitional spaces for inmates progressing toward reintegration.

Open prisons have the **most relaxed conditions**. Inmates often live in dormitory-style accommodations and are permitted to leave the facility daily, returning only at night. Many maintain jobs or take part in educational or vocational training programs in the community. The environment is structured to support reintegration and rehabilitation, with fewer physical security measures and more personal responsibility expected from the inmates. These prisons typically house individuals serving the final part of their sentence or those considered low risk.

Inmates receive **three meals a day**, though the quality and variety of food can differ depending on the facility. **Sanitation** standards also vary. While prisoners are provided with access to showers, toilets, and hygiene supplies, older buildings and overcrowded conditions sometimes lead to complaints about cleanliness and maintenance. Basic needs are met, but the extent to which they are fulfilled can fluctuate with institutional resources and staffing levels.

Spain's prison system continues to struggle with issues like **overcrowding** and **mental health care shortages**. While the government has implemented reforms to align with European human rights standards and promote rehabilitation, progress is uneven across regions. Open prisons have shown promise by reducing recidivism rates, but the broader system still faces structural and operational hurdles.

Inmate Rights and Legal Protections

In Spain, inmates are granted a range of constitutional rights and legal protections, though the effectiveness of these safeguards can vary in practice.

The **Spanish Constitution** and the **General Penitentiary Law** (*Ley Orgánica General Penitenciaria*) affirm **prisoners' rights to life, physical integrity, dignity**, and **equality**. Article 15 of the Constitution prohibits torture and inhumane or degrading treatment, while Article 24 guarantees the right to effective judicial protection, including the right to legal assistance and a fair trial. The General Penitentiary Law further stipulates that prison authorities must protect the life, integrity, and health of prisoners, prohibiting maltreatment by both staff and fellow inmates. (https://defensewiki.ibj.org/index.php/Spain)

Inmates have the **right to access legal resources** and **appeal judicial decisions**. They can **file complaints or requests** directly to a Penitentiary Judge without the need for legal representation. Additionally, the "*recurso de amparo*" allows individuals to appeal to the Constitutional Court if they believe their fundamental rights have been violated, provided all other legal avenues have been exhausted.

Despite these legal frameworks, issues of abuse and inadequate legal recourse persist. Reports from the Council of Europe's Committee for the Prevention of Torture (CPT) have documented allegations of physical ill-treatment by prison officers, including slaps, punches, and kicks, sometimes corroborated by medical records. Furthermore, Amnesty International has raised concerns about "incommunicado" detention practices, where detainees may be held without access to a lawyer of their choice and without private communication, potentially leading to coerced confessions.[40]

While Spain has established protocols for reporting and investigating abuse, such as requiring prison directors to inform judicial authorities of

---

40 https://www.coe.int/en/web/portal/-/cpt-urges-spain-to-prevent-and-effectively-investigate-cases-of-prison-ill-treatment?

alleged mistreatment, the effectiveness of these measures is sometimes questioned. The CPT has criticized the lack of an effective internal complaints system within Spanish prisons, noting issues like the absence of receipts for complaints and undefined timeframes for responses.[41]

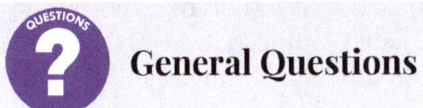

General Questions

1. *Do jails and prisons offer religious services to inmates?*
   Yes. Spanish prisons do offer religious services. The Spanish Constitution protects freedom of religion, and this extends to inmates. Prisoners are entitled to freely practice their religion, provided it does not interfere with the order and security of the prison. The Catholic Church has a long-established presence in the prison system, but other faiths, such as Islam, Protestant Christianity, and Judaism, are also recognized. Religious representatives can visit prisons to lead services or offer personal guidance, and prison authorities are expected to facilitate religious practices, including dietary needs and access to religious texts and materials.

---

41   https://onlinelibrary.wiley.com/doi/full/10.1111/hojo.12585?utm_source

2. *How do prisoners spend their time?* Prisoners in Spain follow a structured daily routine. Time is divided between work assignments, educational programs, rehabilitation workshops, recreational activities, and free time. Many inmates are involved in jobs within the facility such as kitchen duty, laundry, or maintenance. Others may participate in vocational training programs (like carpentry or computer skills) or pursue basic education and even university-level courses. Access to libraries, sports, and outdoor exercise is usually available, although it varies depending on the prison's resources and security level. Inmates in open or semi-open prisons typically have more freedom and may work or study outside the prison during the day, returning in the evening. The system encourages participation in activities as part of the rehabilitation process.

3. *What type of jobs can inmates perform?* Inmates in Spain can take part in various work activities that are designed to support the operation of the facility or to help them gain vocational skills. Common jobs include working in the kitchen, laundry, cleaning, maintenance, carpentry, or gardening. Some prisons also have internal workshops or production facilities where inmates can be employed in manufacturing tasks, such as assembling parts or producing goods for external companies. These jobs are often coordinated by the public company **Trabajo Penitenciario y Formación para el Empleo** (TPFE), which promotes employment and training for inmates. Participation is voluntary, and inmates receive modest wages, part of which may go toward restitution or savings for after release.

4. *How does the prison commissary system work in Spain?* Spanish prisons have a commissary system where inmates can buy items like snacks, toiletries, and tobacco. Purchases are made weekly using funds from prison jobs or deposits from outside. Each inmate has an account, and prices are regulated. Those with no means may receive basic items through assistance programs.

5. ***What type of medical care do prisoners receive?*** Inmates in Spain receive healthcare through prison medical units, which provide basic services including general medicine, nursing, dentistry, and mental health support. For serious conditions or specialist care, inmates are transferred to public hospitals under escort. Challenges remain in mental health care, where resources are often limited, and overcrowding can delay treatment. Medical staff are employed by the prison system, though integration with the public health system (SNS) is ongoing in some regions.

6. ***What is prison culture in Spain?*** Prison culture in Spain varies by facility type and inmate population, but it is generally shaped by a strong emphasis on rehabilitation. Relationships among inmates are typically structured along lines of mutual respect, though tensions can arise, especially in closed prisons. Drug use, though monitored, is still present, and some inmates form informal hierarchies. In open and semi-open prisons, the focus is more on reintegration, with daily routines centered on work, education, and responsibility. Spanish prison culture reflects a broader European model that prioritizes human dignity and social reentry.

HELPING A FRIEND OR RELATIVE IMPRISONED IN SPAIN

HELPING A FRIEND OR RELATIVE IMPRISONED IN SPAIN

Overview

If your family member or friend is imprisoned in Spain, it's important to act quickly and understand the resources available. The first step is to ensure that the detained person requests the prison authorities to **notify the nearest embassy or consulate**. Family members may also contact the **U.S. Embassy in Madrid** or the **Consulate General in Barcelona** directly to inform them of the arrest. The embassy can help by notifying family and friends, facilitating communication, ensuring the detainee's health needs are met, and providing information about the legal process and available local attorneys. While they cannot intervene in legal proceedings or secure a release, they do ensure the detainee's rights are respected.

The embassy provides a **list of English-speaking attorneys** throughout Spain, including Madrid, Barcelona, Valencia, Andalusia, and the Canary Islands. These lawyers are independent and not endorsed by the embassy, but they are available to represent foreign nationals in criminal proceedings.

 This list can be found on the U.S. Embassy's official legal assistance page at **https://es.usembassy.gov/ legal-assistance**.

In certain emergency situations, the U.S. government may provide limited financial support, such as loans for repatriation or medical emergencies. The embassy also offers help to victims of crime who are imprisoned, including referrals to local shelters and legal aid when needed.

You can support your relative or friend detained in Spain in several other ways. Maintaining regular communication is essential—**writing letters** or **speaking by phone** helps provide emotional stability and keeps them connected to the outside world. Depending on the facility, inmates may also have access to **video calls** or **email**. **Financial assistance** can also be crucial. Sending money allows your loved one to purchase food, hygiene items, and other essentials through the prison commissary. This can be done by transferring funds to their inmate account or, for U.S. citizens, through an OCS Trust set up via the embassy.[42]

Visiting the prisoner is often allowed but subject to facility rules. Visits typically must be arranged in advance and require valid identification. Personal visits can be a powerful source of encouragement and connection. In some cases, you may also **send packages** containing books, clothing, or approved personal items, but this is regulated and should be coordinated with the specific prison.

Beyond these direct supports, you can advocate on their behalf if you believe their rights are being violated. Reaching out to **human rights organizations** such as **Rights International Spain**[43] can help in cases involving mistreatment, unfair detention, or legal missteps.

Sending Food, Supplies, and Money to an Inmate

In Spain, family and friends are **not allowed to bring or send food directly to inmates**. Prisons provide regular meals, and inmates can supplement their diet by purchasing food items through the internal commissary. In some facilities, inmates are allowed to make purchases from

---

42 https://usacs-info.com/en-es/topics/us-citizen-arrest/
person_in_country_prison_help

43 https://www.rightsinternationalspain.org

outside supermarkets once a month or weekly, depending on institutional policy.[44]

Packages can be sent to inmates, but **strict regulations apply**. Each inmate is generally allowed to receive and send **only one package per month**. Packages must be sent through approved postal services, and in many cases, the prison must be informed in advance about the contents and the shipment. Items considered dangerous, such as weapons, illegal substances, and electronic devices like mobile phones, are strictly prohibited.[45, 46].

Money can be sent to inmates through two main methods. The first is a **bank transfer** to the prison's financial department, known as *"peculio."* The sender must include the inmate's full name and prison number (NIS) in the transfer details, and only authorized individuals such as verified family members or legal representatives may send money. Identification and proof of relationship are often required, and prisons generally limit the number of deposits to two per month. The second method is through **MyTelio**, a service that allows deposits ranging from €10 to €30 (US$11 to $33), which can be used by the inmate for telephone calls. This service requires the inmate's NIS number and an authorized phone number.[47]

Mail, Phone Calls, and Visitation

In Spain, inmates are allowed to receive mail, including letters and photographs. All incoming and outgoing mail is **subject to inspection** for

---

44 https://www.icpo.ie/imprisoned-in-spain

45 https://www.interior.gob.es/opencms/pdf/archivos-y-documentacion/documentacion-y-publicaciones/publicaciones-descargables/instituciones-penitenciarias/Prison_step_by_step-La-prision-paso-a-paso-NIPO-126-10-134-8.pdf

46 https://www.eurosender.com/en/cp/care-package/prison

47 https://www.mytelio.es, https://www.gov.uk/government/publications/spain-prisoner-pack/british-prisoners-pack

security reasons. Letters are opened and inspected in the presence of the inmate, and prohibited items such as bracelets or unauthorized documents are not permitted. There is no official limit on the number of letters an inmate can send or receive; however, restrictions may apply if deemed necessary for security or institutional order.[48]

Inmates are not permitted to possess personal cell phones. They can make phone calls using the **prison's telephone system**, which is typically operated by a single provider. The number of calls an inmate can make per week varies; somewhere between two and five, depending on the institution's capacity. Calls are generally made **collect or pre-paid**, and the cost can be higher than standard rates due to the monopoly of the service provider.

Visitation rules in Spanish prisons vary by facility. Generally, inmates are allowed between **four to eight visits per month**, with each visit lasting between 20 and 40 minutes. Intimate visits, which allow for private contact, are permitted at least once per month and can last between one to three hours. Family visits, without ordinary exit permits, are also allowed for one to three hours per month. Additionally, quarterly coexistence visits of four to six hours are possible, especially for inmates with children under 10 years old.[49]

It's important to note that these **policies can vary between different prisons** in Spain, and specific rules should be confirmed with the individual institution.

Prison Scams

Prison scams in Spain can take many forms, and it's important to be aware of the different tactics used by scammers. One common scam involves **emergency calls from prisoners**, where scammers impersonate

---

48 https://expatsmagazine.org/has-a-family-member-or-friend-been-de-tained-under-the-european-arrest-warrant/

49 https://childrenofprisoners.eu/facts_and_figures/
visits-allowed-per-month

a prisoner and claim to be in urgent need of financial assistance for medical fees, legal costs, or other emergency situations. Another frequent scam is when **individuals posing as lawyers** offer to help reduce a prisoner's sentence or secure their release, often asking for upfront payments. Similarly, scammers may claim that a package is waiting for the prisoner and request a fee to deliver it, promising special privileges or items that aren't typically available.

Phishing emails or social media scams also occur, where individuals pretending to be prison officials or even the prisoners themselves ask for money to send mail, gifts, or communications. Additionally, some **scammers impersonate family members or friends** of prisoners, asking for money to cover essentials or emotional support.

Red flags to watch out for include any sense of urgency created by the scammer, who may claim that immediate action is required to avoid harm or solve a problem. If the contact is from an unverifiable source or you have not been previously informed about the situation, this could indicate a scam. Unsolicited requests for money, especially when the person contacting you is someone you weren't expecting to hear from, should be approached with caution. Also, if the request involves unusual payment methods like wire transfers, gift cards, or cryptocurrency, it's a strong sign of a scam. Lastly, if the details provided by the scammer don't align with known facts or raise inconsistencies with the prisoner's actual situation, it's essential to verify the information.

If you suspect you are being scammed, it's crucial to **stop communication immediately** and **verify the situation by contacting the prison directly** through official channels. To report the scam, you can reach out to the Spanish National Police or Guardia Civil. They have official websites where you can file complaints and get more information on how to protect yourself. If any financial information was shared, **contact your bank right away** to secure your accounts. Additionally, educating others about these scams can help prevent further victims. Resources like **Bitdefender** and **Pineradelolmo** provide advice on reporting cybercrime and handling fraud in Spain. By staying informed and cautious, you can protect yourself and others from falling victim to these scams.

Upon Release

When a foreign national is released from prison in Spain, there are several **legal considerations and rules** they must adhere to, which may vary depending on their specific circumstances. While the general rules for individuals released from Spanish prisons apply to both nationals and foreigners, there are additional obligations or restrictions that can be imposed on foreigners.

One of the key considerations is that, if the foreigner does not have legal residency status in Spain, they may be subject to **deportation** or **required to leave the country** once their sentence is completed. This decision is typically made by immigration authorities, who assess whether the individual is allowed to stay in Spain or must return to their home country. In some cases, the individual may be granted temporary permission to stay in Spain, particularly if they have family or other ties in the country.

Foreign nationals released from prison in Spain may also face additional **reporting obligations** to immigration authorities. This can involve regular check-ins with the police or immigration officials to ensure they comply with the terms of their release. Depending on the individual's legal status, restrictions may be imposed, such as travel bans or limits on their ability to work or access public services. If the person is facing deportation, the authorities may also impose measures like electronic monitoring or residence restrictions while they await deportation proceedings.

In addition, if the person has committed a serious crime or is considered a high-risk individual, there may be additional legal measures such as **parole restrictions** or specific conditions related to their reintegration into society. For example, they might be required to attend rehabilitation programs, undergo regular drug testing, or avoid certain areas or people. Furthermore, foreign nationals released from prison in Spain may encounter challenges in obtaining work or accessing social services, depending on their residency status. If the individual's residence permit was revoked during their imprisonment, they might need to apply for re-entry or special residency status to remain in Spain legally.

To navigate these obligations, foreigners are often **advised to seek legal counsel** to understand their rights and ensure compliance with both criminal and immigration laws after their release. Additionally, they may need to coordinate with local legal aid organizations or support groups to facilitate their reintegration and manage any legal obligations or restrictions.

THE ADMINISTRATION OF JUSTICE

THE ADMINISTRATION OF JUSTICE

Spain's Legal System

Spain's legal system is rooted in the **Roman law tradition**, which has deeply influenced the structure and principles of modern civil law systems across much of continental Europe. Roman legal principles were adopted during the Roman Empire's control of the Iberian Peninsula and continued to shape Spanish legal codes through the Middle Ages. In the 19th century, Spain codified its laws under the **Civil Code of 1889**, heavily influenced by the Napoleonic Code. This codification marked the formal transition into a modern civil law system. A major turning point came after the death of dictator Francisco Franco in 1975. Spain transitioned to a constitutional democracy with the ratification of the **Spanish Constitution of 1978**, which established the current legal and political framework and remains the supreme legal authority in the country.[50]

The key components of Spain's legal system include **the Constitution**, which defines the structure of government, fundamental rights, and the separation of powers; **the Civil Code**, which governs areas such as contracts, property, and family law; **the Criminal Code**, which outlines offenses and penalties; and various codes regulating labor, administrative,

---

50   https://www.boe.es/

and commercial law. Spanish law is primarily codified, meaning judges rely more on **statutes** than on judicial precedent when making decisions. While judicial decisions are respected, they do not create binding case law as in common law systems.

Spain's judiciary is **hierarchical** and divided into several levels. At the top is the **Supreme Court** (*Tribunal Supremo*), the highest ordinary court in Spain, which handles appeals and oversees civil, criminal, administrative, and labor law cases. Separately, the **Constitutional Court** (*Tribunal Constitucional*) interprets the Constitution and has the authority to strike down laws that violate it. Below these are the **High Courts of Justice** (*Tribunales Superiores de Justicia*) in each autonomous community, which handle regional matters. **Provincial Courts** (*Audiencias Provinciales*) deal with appeals from lower courts, and **lower courts** (*Juzgados de Primera Instancia e Instrucción*) handle first-instance civil and criminal cases. There are also specialized courts for issues like labor law, administrative disputes, gender violence, and minors.[51]

Distinctive features of Spain's judiciary include its constitutional commitment to judicial independence and the role of the **General Council of the Judiciary** (*Consejo General del Poder Judicial*), which governs the judiciary, appoints judges, and ensures independence from the executive and legislative branches. Spain also has a decentralized structure, allowing autonomous communities to manage some aspects of judicial administration. Additionally, the **Constitutional Court** plays a powerful role, separate from the regular judicial system, with the exclusive ability to rule on constitutional matters.[52]

Spain's judiciary faces a number of challenges. One of the most persistent is **court backlogs and delays**, particularly in civil and administrative courts, which can result in cases taking years to resolve. Another major issue is the **politicization of judicial appointments**, especially to the Constitutional Court and the General Council of the Judiciary, where the nomination process is often influenced by political parties, undermining

---

51 https://www.poderjudicial.es/cgpj/

52 https://www.tribunalconstitucional.es/en/Paginas/default.aspx

public confidence in judicial neutrality. Spain also struggles with **corruption cases** involving political or business elites, which are sometimes perceived as handled unevenly or slowly. These challenges have prompted criticism from civil society and international organizations about the need to ensure transparency, efficiency, and independence.[53]

 **General Questions**

1. *Will the court treat first-time offenders and tourists with more leniency?* In Spain, courts may show some leniency to first-time offenders, especially if the offense is minor, the person shows remorse or cooperates with authorities. The Penal Code allows reduced penalties in such cases, though it's not guaranteed. Tourists aren't automatically treated more leniently, but factors like unfamiliarity with local laws or cooperation might be considered. However, being a foreigner can sometimes work against a defendant—such as increasing the risk of pretrial detention if the court sees a flight risk. Ultimately, outcomes depend on the specific details of each case.

2. *If I am charged with a crime, which court is likely to hear my case?* If you are charged with a crime in Spain, your case will most likely be heard by a **Juzgado de Instrucción** (Investigating Court) and then a **Juzgado de lo Penal** (Criminal Court) or an **Audiencia Provincial** (Provincial Court), depending on the seriousness of the offense. For minor to moderate crimes (with penalties under five years), the **Criminal Court** will handle the trial. For more serious offenses, especially those involving violence or longer potential sentences, the **Provincial Court** will take the case. The **Investigating Court** is always the first step—it handles the initial investigation, decides on pretrial measures, and refers the case to the appropriate trial court.

---

53 https://elpais.com/us/

3. ***What is the standard of proof in a criminal case in Spain?*** In Spain, the standard of proof in a criminal case is *"más allá de toda duda razonable"*—beyond a reasonable doubt. This means the judge or panel of judges must be fully convinced of the defendant's guilt based on the evidence presented. Since Spain does not use jury trials for most cases, it is typically judges who evaluate the facts, witness testimony, and legal arguments to determine if the prosecution has met this high standard before delivering a guilty verdict.

 **Law of the Land True Story**[54]

In 2017, Spain's Supreme Court confirmed the 21-month prison sentence for Lionel Messi after he and his father were found guilty of defrauding the Spanish tax authorities of over €4 million (approximately US$4.5 million). Though neither served jail time due to Spanish law allowing sentences under two years to be suspended, the case became a powerful moment in the public eye—one where a global superstar was tried and sentenced by the same system that governs ordinary citizens.

This case offers a sharp lens through which to view the functioning of the Spanish judiciary. On the one hand, it reinforced the idea of equality before the law. Messi's fame and success did not shield him from prosecution, and the Spanish legal system showed itself capable of pursuing high-profile financial crimes. On the other hand, the case exposed common criticisms: the slow pace of judicial proceedings, the perception that wealth can buy softer outcomes, and broader concerns about transparency and consistency.

---

54 https://www.bbc.com/news/world-europe-40026827

Takeaways

- Spain's legal system is based on Roman law and was modernized through the Civil Code of 1889 and the 1978 Constitution, which established the current democratic legal framework.

- The judiciary is structured hierarchically, with the Supreme Court and Constitutional Court at the top, supported by regional and specialized courts handling civil, criminal, and administrative cases.

- Major challenges include slow proceedings, court backlogs, and concerns about fairness and transparency, especially in politically sensitive or high-profile cases.

- First-time offenders may receive reduced sentences under Spanish law, but tourists are not automatically treated more leniently and may even face stricter pretrial conditions due to flight risk.

- Spain uses the "beyond a reasonable doubt" standard in criminal cases, and the Lionel Messi tax fraud case demonstrated both the system's commitment to legal equality and ongoing public concerns.

CRIME VICTIM ASSISTANCE

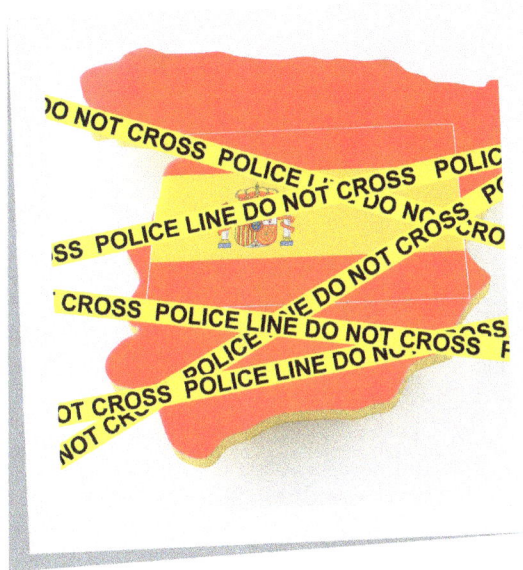

CRIME VICTIM ASSISTANCE

Overview

Crime victims in Spain have access to a range of resources, both through government services and non-governmental organizations. The Spanish government provides free **Victim Support Offices** (*Oficinas de Asistencia a las Víctimas del Delito*) throughout the country. These offices offer legal guidance, psychological support, and help navigating the judicial process. Services are confidential and available to all victims, including foreigners and tourists.

 You can locate your nearest Victim Support Office through the Ministry of Justice website at **www.mjusticia. gob.es.**

In addition to government services, several non-governmental organizations support victims of crime. Organizations such as **Fundación ANAR** assist child and adolescent victims, while **APRAMP** helps victims of trafficking and exploitation. Other groups like **Cruz Roja Española** (Red Cross Spain) and **CEAR** (Spanish Commission for Refugee Aid) offer emergency shelter, counseling, and legal aid, especially to vulnerable populations.

Emergency assistance is available via Spain's national emergency number **112**, which can connect callers to police, medical help, and fire services. For gender-based violence, victims can call **016**, a 24/7 confidential helpline that does not appear on phone bills. These resources ensure that victims can access help quickly and safely across the country.

What to Do If You Are the Victim of a Crime

If you become a victim of crime in Spain, your first step should be to ensure your safety and call **112**, the national emergency number, for immediate assistance from police, medical services, or firefighters. If the situation is not urgent but still serious, go to the nearest **police station** (*Comisaría de Policía* or *Guardia Civil*) to file a formal complaint (*denuncia*), which is necessary for launching an investigation. You can request an interpreter if you don't speak Spanish.

After reporting, you can contact a **Victim Support Office** (*Oficina de Asistencia a las Víctimas del Delito*) for free legal and psychological help, regardless of your nationality. These offices guide you through the legal process and provide emotional support. You may also reach out to NGOs like the **Red Cross**, **CEAR**, or **Fundación ANAR**, depending on the type of crime and your needs.

Keep all documentation—including the police report, medical records, and any communication with authorities—as it may be needed for legal proceedings or insurance claims. If your passport or ID was stolen, contact your embassy or consulate immediately to arrange replacements.

Common Tourist Scams in Spain

Common scams targeting tourists in Spain include **pickpocketing** in crowded areas, especially in cities like Barcelona and Madrid. Thieves often work in groups and use distractions like someone "accidentally" bumping into you or spilling something on your clothes while another person steals your belongings. **Fake petition scams** are also common— someone may ask you to sign a petition for a charity or cause, using the moment to pick your pocket or pressure you for money. In some tourist areas, people may offer **unsolicited help** at ticket machines or ATMs and then demand a tip or attempt to steal your card information.

Other scams include the **"friendship bracelet" trick**, where someone places a bracelet on your wrist and then demands payment, or street performers and buskers who aggressively solicit tips. Fake police officers have also been reported—scammers posing as plainclothes officers ask to see your ID or wallet to "check for counterfeit money" and then take your cash.

To avoid these scams, stay alert in crowded areas, keep your valuables secure and out of sight, be wary of unsolicited help or overly friendly strangers, and never hand over your wallet—ask any police officer for ID and insist on going to the nearest station if unsure. **Trust your instincts: if something feels off or too persistent, it probably is.**

Sexual Assault

If you are a victim of sexual assault in Spain, your immediate priority should be safety. Call **112** for emergency assistance or go directly to the nearest hospital or police station. Spanish authorities take sexual violence seriously, and there are established procedures to support victims medically, legally, and emotionally. You do not need to file a police report immediately in order to receive medical attention or support services.

To report the incident, you can go to a **police station** (*Policía Nacional* or *Guardia Civil*) or ask hospital staff to notify police for you. If you prefer, you can request to speak with a **female officer** and ask for a translator if needed. Filing a report (*denuncia*) initiates a legal process and preserves evidence for possible prosecution. Medical exams are conducted with consent and are important for both health and legal reasons.[55]

As a victim, you have the right to **free legal aid**, access to a **psychologist**, a translator, and support from **Victim Assistance Offices** (*Oficinas de Asistencia a las Víctimas del Delito*). You may also receive a protection

---

55 https://www.policia.es/_es/vio_ayuda_victimas.php

order if there is ongoing danger. Your identity is protected, and you cannot be forced to face your aggressor during testimony.[56]

For safety, avoid isolated areas at night, be cautious with alcohol or drink offers from strangers, and keep your phone charged and location shared with a trusted person when going out. If you are a victim of sexual assault in Spain, remember that you are not alone. The legal system and support services are designed to protect your rights and provide the assistance you need. No matter your nationality or background, you have the right to feel safe, respected, and supported.

Consular Assistance

If you are a victim of a crime in Spain, your embassy or consulate can provide essential support. They can offer emergency assistance, such as helping you replace a lost or stolen passport, arranging for emergency travel documents, and notifying family members if necessary. They can also assist you in finding a local lawyer and provide guidance on the Spanish legal process. However, while consulates can inform you about the legal system and available services, they cannot represent you in court or intervene directly in legal matters.

Embassies are also equipped to connect you with victim support services, such as emergency shelters, crisis hotlines, and mental health resources. If you are not fluent in Spanish, consular staff can assist with translation, ensuring you can communicate effectively with local authorities and support organizations. Furthermore, if you need to return to your home country due to the crime, they can provide information on repatriation options and help you arrange transportation if needed.

That being said, there are limitations to consular assistance. Embassies cannot represent you legally, influence the outcome of a legal case, or intervene in the Spanish justice system. Additionally, consulates do not provide direct financial assistance or compensation for victims of crime. They can, however, help you navigate available local resources.

---

56 https://www.mjusticia.gob.es

For assistance, you can contact your embassy or consulate directly. Contact information for embassies in Spain can typically be found on their respective websites or through the Spanish Ministry of Foreign Affairs at **https://www. exteriores.gob.es**.

General Questions

1. *If I am a victim of a crime, can I legally be compensated?*
   Yes. Victims of crime in Spain may be entitled to compensation. The **Victims of Crime Compensation Fund** offers financial support for personal injury or property damage resulting from violent crimes, covering expenses like medical bills, lost income, and funeral costs. To be eligible, victims must report the crime to the police and pursue legal action. If the perpetrator is identified but unable to pay, the fund can still provide compensation. Victims may also seek civil compensation through the courts as part of criminal proceedings. It's important to report the crime and seek guidance from victim support services to navigate the compensation process.

2. *Are there any special considerations or rights for tourists who become victims of crimes in Spain?* **Yes.** Tourists who become victims of crime in Spain have the right to report the crime to the police and access victim support services, such as the **Oficina de Atención a las Víctimas del Delito** (Victim Assistance Offices), which offer legal guidance, psychological support, and information on their rights. Police officers can provide assistance in multiple languages and arrange translation services if needed. Tourists can also contact their embassy or consulate for help with replacing lost passports, emergency travel documents, or contacting family members, although embassies cannot intervene in legal matters. Victims have the right to be informed of their case's progress and can attend court hearings if necessary. If the crime involves personal injury, tourists may be eligible for compensation for medical costs, lost income, and other damages.

3. *What should a traveler do if they lose their passport or important documents while in Spain after becoming a victim of crime?* If a traveler loses their passport or important documents in Spain after becoming a victim of crime, the first step is to report the loss to the local police and obtain a police report, which may be needed for insurance or a replacement passport. Next, contact your embassy or consulate, which can issue an emergency travel document or temporary passport, and assist with other documentation like a visa or re-entry permit. It's also important to monitor for identity theft if personal items were stolen, notifying your bank and credit card companies to block or cancel compromised cards. Additionally, you can access **Victim Assistance Offices** for support, including legal guidance and help with documentation.

 **Safety Tips**

- **Stay alert in crowded areas:** Tourist-heavy zones like train stations, metro lines, markets, and landmarks are prime spots for pickpockets. Keep your bags zipped and close to your body, and avoid carrying valuables in easily accessible pockets.

- **Be cautious with strangers:** Politely decline offers of help from overly friendly individuals, especially around ATMs, train ticket machines, or major attractions. Don't accept gifts, petitions, or bracelets from street vendors unless you intend to pay.

- **Use only official taxis and rideshares:** Avoid unlicensed taxis, especially those waiting near airports or nightlife areas. Official taxis in Spain have meters and identification cards displayed inside.

- **Avoid isolated areas at night:** Stick to well-lit streets and busy neighborhoods after dark, especially when walking alone. When in doubt, take a licensed taxi or ride-share service back to your accommodation.

- **Keep emergency numbers handy:** Save Spain's emergency number (112) and the number of your country's embassy or consulate in your phone. For gender-based violence, dial 016—a free, confidential helpline that does not show up on phone bills.

- **Trust your instincts:** If something feels off—whether it's a pushy salesperson, a suspicious person watching you, or someone posing as police—leave the area and seek help. Real police officers carry ID and will not ask to inspect your wallet on the street without cause.

CHAPTER 15

POLICE

IN THIS CHAPTER

- Overview
- Police Response
- Police and Community Relations
- Police Use of Force
- Law of the Land True Story

CHAPTER 15

POLICE

Overview

Spain's police system is structured across three main levels: national, regional, and local. At the national level, there are two primary forces— the **Policía Nacional** and the **Guardia Civil**. Some autonomous regions have their own regional police forces, which handle most policing duties in their territories. Additionally, **local or municipal police** (*Policía Local*) are present in towns and cities.

As of recent data, Spain has around **240,000 law enforcement personnel** across all branches, with approximately **68,000 in the Policía Nacional, 78,000 in the Guardia Civil**, and the remainder split among regional and local police forces. Spain has one of the higher police-to-population ratios in Europe, with about **3.7 police officers per 1,000 residents**, slightly above the EU average.[57]

While Spain's police force is generally considered well-staffed, there are ongoing concerns about **uneven staffing across regions**, especially in rural areas or during high tourism seasons. Some local forces report shortages that impact response times or coverage, while others experience high demand due to protests, public events, or immigration pressures.

---

57 https://as.com/diarioas/2021/11/28/actualidad/1638105947_403321. html?utm_source

Despite this, Spain maintains strong public safety and is viewed as having a relatively effective and professional police system.[58]

Police Response

As mentioned above, Spain's police system operates across national, regional, and local levels, each with distinct responsibilities. The **Policía Nacional** primarily handles criminal investigations, terrorism, immigration, and passport control in urban areas. The **Guardia Civil**, a military police force, is responsible for rural areas, border control, highway patrol, and civil order. A few autonomous regions, like Catalonia and the Basque Country, have their own regional police forces, such as the **Mossos d'Esquadra** and **Ertzaintza**, which manage most policing duties in their territories. Additionally, **local or municipal police** (*Policía Local*) operate in towns and cities, focusing on traffic, public order, and enforcing local laws.

The primary functions of these law enforcement agencies include maintaining public order, preventing and investigating crimes, ensuring road safety, and protecting citizens' rights. They also collaborate with the judiciary and other institutions to uphold the rule of law.[59]

However, Spain's police forces face **several challenges**. Issues such as allegations of excessive use of force, particularly during public demonstrations, have raised concerns. For instance, in 2017, reports emerged of the National Police and Civil Guard using disproportionate force during events in Catalonia. Additionally, incidents of racial profiling and discrimination have been reported, highlighting the need for improved training and oversight.[60]

---

58 https://english.elpais.com/elpais/2018/02/27/inenglish/1519721826_405189.html?utm_source

59 https://www.lamoncloa.gob.es/lang/en/espana/stpv/spaintoday2015/security/paginas/index.aspx?

60 https://www.amnesty.org/en/latest/press-release/2017/10/spain-excessive-use-of-force-by-national-police-and-civil-guard-in-catalonia/

In response to these challenges, Spain has initiated several **reforms**. Efforts include revising police protocols to ensure better adherence to human rights standards and implementing training programs focused on diversity and non-discrimination. Moreover, there is an ongoing push to enhance transparency and accountability within law enforcement agencies. While these reforms signify progress, continuous evaluation and adaptation are essential to address the evolving needs of society and to maintain public trust in law enforcement institutions.

Police and Community Relations

In Spain, the overall public perception of the police is relatively positive, with **law enforcement considered one of the more trusted public institutions**. A 2024 OECD survey found that 61 percent of Spaniards expressed a high or moderately high level of trust in the police, placing it above many other government bodies in terms of public confidence.[61] Similarly, YouGov data indicated that 67 percent of Spaniards believe the police are effective at dealing with crime, and 76 percent said police do a good job overall.[62]

Despite these favorable views, concerns remain about certain practices, particularly among minority communities. Reports by organizations like the Open Society Justice Initiative have pointed to patterns of **ethnic profiling**, where individuals from marginalized groups are disproportionately stopped by police.[63] These practices can undermine trust, especially in neighborhoods where residents already feel over-policed or unfairly treated.

---

61   https://www.oecd.org/en/publications/oecd-survey-on-drivers-of-trust-in-public-institutions-2024-results-country-notes_a8004759-en/spain_56998449-en.html

62   https://yougov.co.uk/politics/articles/42510-how-do-western-european-and-us-perceptions-crime-a

63   https://www.justiceinitiative.org/uploads/21ac6560-639d-461c-a6b7-06822ad1c07e/under-suspicion-the-impact-of-discriminatory-policing-in-spain-20190924.pdf

In response, civil society groups and human rights advocates have pushed for stronger safeguards and oversight mechanisms. Some regional police forces, like the Mossos d'Esquadra in Catalonia, have taken steps to implement body cameras and community outreach initiatives, aiming to promote transparency and improve dialogue between officers and the public. National discussions about reforming stop-and-search procedures and increasing accountability are also underway. At the heart of these efforts is the recognition that fair, respectful, and non-discriminatory policing is essential to building lasting trust across all segments of society. Improving communication, ensuring proportionality in policing, and expanding training in diversity and human rights are seen as vital measures.

Police Use of Force

The use of force by police in Spain has been a contentious issue, with several high-profile incidents drawing national and international scrutiny. One of the most notable cases occurred during the Catalan independence referendum on October 1, 2017. Human Rights Watch documented instances where the Spanish National Police and Civil Guard used excessive force against peaceful demonstrators, including hitting non-threatening protesters with batons, resulting in numerous injuries. Amnesty International also reported similar findings, highlighting the disproportionate use of force by law enforcement during the referendum. As of January 2023, 45 National Police officers were facing potential trials for their alleged actions during this event.[64] There are numerous other more recent examples, too. (See *Law of the Land True Story* below.)

These incidents underscore ongoing concerns about police conduct in Spain, particularly regarding the use of excessive force and the treatment of minority communities. While some efforts have been made to address these issues, such as investigations and potential trials, critics argue that

---

64 https://www.theolivepress.es/spain-news/2023/01/25/five-years-later-45-national-police-officers-could-face-trial-for-excessive-force-at-illegal-catalan-independence-referendum/

more comprehensive reforms are necessary to ensure accountability and prevent future abuses.

Law of the Land True Story[65]

The 2022 incident at Spain's Melilla border raised serious concerns about the use of force by Spanish police against migrants. A widely circulated video showed police officers beating and pepper-spraying a sub-Saharan African man as he attempted to scale the border fence, sparking public outrage and condemnation from human rights groups. Despite the backlash, Spain's interior minister Fernando Grande-Marlaska defended the officers' actions as "proportionate," citing the aggressive tactics used by some migrants, including the use of meat hooks and makeshift tools.

Human rights organizations, such as Amnesty International and Andalucía's Pro-Human Rights Association, criticized the apparent brutality, especially in contrast to Spain's simultaneous efforts to welcome Ukrainian refugees. Spain's public ombudsman called for an investigation into the "disproportionate use of force" and stressed the need for border enforcement that respects fundamental human rights.

The incident highlighted a deeper tension in Spain's immigration and border policy—balancing security and humanitarian obligations. It also intensified debates around the treatment of African migrants and the inconsistent response to different migrant groups, revealing ongoing challenges in the country's approach to border control and police accountability.

---

65 https://www.theguardian.com/world/2022/mar/06/
    spanish-minister-defends-police-accused-brutality-melilla-border

HOW TO GET LEGAL HELP IN SPAIN

HOW TO GET LEGAL HELP IN SPAIN

Available Resources

If you are arrested in Spain or need legal help, it's important to know where to turn for reliable assistance. The police are required to inform you of your right to legal representation. You have the right to contact a lawyer immediately. If you cannot afford a lawyer, you are entitled to a public defender.

To find reliable legal representation, you can ask the police for a list of lawyers, or you can contact the **Spanish Bar Association** (*Consejo General de la Abogacía Española*), which can provide referrals to qualified attorneys. Many lawyers in Spain speak English, so you should be able to find one who can communicate with you in your preferred language.

Consulates or embassies also provide resources for foreigners. Many consulates have lists of local attorneys that speak your language and are familiar with the legal system. You can usually access these lists on the consulate's website. It's recommended to reach out to your embassy or consulate as soon as possible after an arrest, as they can offer support, assist with communication, and help you understand the legal process in Spain.

For emergency assistance, organizations like the **Red Cross** (*Cruz Roja*) and **local NGOs** provide help to people in legal trouble, including victims of crime or those in detention. They can offer support, translation services, and legal referrals. In case you need help navigating the system, it's also advisable to contact local legal aid services if available in your region.

Legal Aid

Foreign visitors in Spain are eligible for legal aid if they meet **specific criteria**. Legal aid is available to both Spanish and foreign citizens, including non-EU nationals, provided they can demonstrate that they lack sufficient financial resources.[66] This also applies to individuals involved in criminal, civil, administrative, and labor law proceedings, and those who are victims of certain crimes such as gender violence, terrorism, or human trafficking.

To apply for legal aid, applicants must contact the local **Bar Association** (*Colegio de Abogados*), where a **Legal Advice Service** (*Servicio de Orientación Jurídica*) will assist them in the application process. The applicant must provide documentation such as proof of identity, evidence of income and assets, and relevant legal case documents. The application is reviewed by a commission which determines eligibility based on economic criteria and the nature of the case.[67]

The eligibility criteria are focused on **financial need**. Applicants must prove they cannot afford legal representation. Factors such as monthly income, household composition, and financial liabilities are evaluated. Some groups, such as victims of domestic violence, may be automatically entitled to legal aid without a financial assessment.[68]

---

66 https://www.gov.uk/government/publications/legal-aid-in-spain/legal-aid-in-spain

67 https://www.abogacia.es/en/areas-tematicas/justicia-gratuita/

68 https://www.gov.uk/government/publications/legal-aid-in-spain/legal-aid-in-spain)

Legal aid in Spain includes **initial legal advice, representation by a lawyer** and court procurator where necessary, coverage of **court fees** and **costs related to expert witnesses or reports**, and in some cases, a **reduction in administrative fees** for official certifications and public deeds.[69]

Foreign Embassies in Spain

Embassies and consulates serve distinct yet complementary roles in international diplomacy. **Embassies**, typically located in a nation's capital, are led by ambassadors and handle high-level diplomatic relations, policy discussions, and represent their home country's interests to the host government. **Consulates**, on the other hand, are situated in major cities and focus on providing services to citizens abroad, such as issuing passports, assisting in emergencies, and facilitating trade and cultural exchanges.

As of 2024, Spain is home to 126 resident embassies, all situated in Madrid. Additionally, there are nearly 800 consular offices across the country, comprising 153 official consulates-general and over 600 honorary consulates. These missions are distributed throughout major cities such as Barcelona, Valencia, Seville, Málaga, Bilbao, and the Canary and Balearic Islands.

Prominent embassies in Madrid include those of the United Kingdom, Germany, France, China, and Russia. These embassies play crucial roles in diplomatic relations, trade negotiations, cultural exchanges, and providing services to their nationals. The United States maintains a significant diplomatic presence in Spain, with its embassy located in Madrid and consulates in Barcelona and Palma de Mallorca. These missions provide services including visa processing, assistance to U.S. citizens, and fostering bilateral relations.

69 https://www.abogacia.es/en/servicios/ciudadanos/
servicios-de-orientacion-juridica-gratuita/

 For a comprehensive list of foreign embassies and consulates in Spain, you can refer to the official Spanish government directory at **www.exteriores.gob.es/en/ EmbajadasConsulados/Paginas/index.asp.**

 Additionally, the U.S. Department of State provides information on U.S. embassies and consulates worldwide at **www.usembassy.gov.**

MEDICAL FACILITIES & HOSPITALS

MEDICAL FACILITIES & HOSPITALS

Overview

Spain's healthcare system is widely regarded as **one of the best in the world**, known for its high efficiency, accessibility, and quality of care. The country offers a public healthcare system called the **Sistema Nacional de Salud** (**SNS**), which provides universal coverage to Spanish citizens and residents. This system is funded primarily through taxation and includes general practitioner services, hospital care, emergency services, and specialist treatments.

Public healthcare is available to residents, including European Union citizens with an EHIC card, and non-EU residents who contribute to social security or have become legal residents. Private healthcare exists alongside the public system and is often used for quicker access to specialists and reduced wait times. Many Spaniards and expats choose to complement the public system with **private insurance**, which is relatively affordable.

In terms of accessibility, nearly every town and city in Spain has public health centers (*centros de salud*) and hospitals, making medical care easy to reach for most people. The quality of care is high, with a focus on preventive services, chronic disease management, and modern medical facilities. Public healthcare is either free or involves minimal co-payments, especially for prescriptions, which are subsidized by the government.

This affordability makes the Spanish healthcare system one of the most cost-effective in Europe.[70]

For **emergencies**, Spain uses the EU-wide number **112**, which connects callers to police, fire, and medical services. There is also a dedicated **medical emergency number**, **061**, available in most regions for direct medical assistance. Some regional health services also offer non-emergency medical advice lines, though these vary by area.

Visitors' Access to Healthcare in Spain

All visitors to Spain have access to medical services, but the way they receive and pay for care depends on their country of origin and their insurance coverage. Citizens from European Union (EU) or European Economic Area (EEA) countries can access public healthcare services in Spain through the **European Health Insurance Card (EHIC)**. This card entitles them to necessary healthcare during a temporary stay, under the same conditions and at the same cost as residents of Spain. This means that visits to a public doctor or hospital are typically free or come with only a small co-payment, depending on the treatment and the region.[71]

Non-EU visitors, including travelers from the United States, Canada, Australia, and other countries, are generally not entitled to use the public healthcare system for free unless they become legal residents or have special reciprocal agreements in place. These travelers are advised—and often required by visa rules—to purchase **private travel health insurance** before arriving in Spain. In the event of illness or injury, they can access care through public hospitals by paying out of pocket, or they can choose private healthcare providers, which may offer shorter wait times and more personalized services. Private medical care in Spain is known for being more affordable than in many other countries, although it is still significantly more expensive than the subsidized public system. Having comprehensive travel insurance ensures that visitors are reimbursed or covered for the cost of treatment.

---

70 https://www.oecd.org/spain/health/

71 https://ec.europa.eu/social/main.jsp?catId=559

Language barriers can present challenges, especially in emergency situations or in rural areas where English is less commonly spoken. While many healthcare professionals in Spain receive basic English training, fluency is not guaranteed across the board. In major cities like Madrid, Barcelona, Valencia, and in coastal areas popular with tourists, many doctors, nurses, and hospital staff speak English or other languages, and some clinics cater specifically to international patients. Private hospitals and international clinics are more likely to have multilingual staff, including English-speaking doctors, receptionists, and interpreters. Still, in smaller towns or non-tourist areas, it can be harder to find English-speaking healthcare providers, which can lead to communication difficulties. For this reason, travelers are encouraged to carry their health records or important medical information translated into Spanish, use translation apps, or contact their consulate for assistance if they need help navigating the healthcare system.[72]

Spain's Hospitals

Spain has an extensive healthcare infrastructure with approximately **450 public hospitals** and over **300 private hospitals**, totaling more than **750 hospitals nationwide**.[73] The healthcare workforce is also robust, with over **790,000 healthcare professionals**, including doctors, nurses, specialists, and technicians, working across the public and private sectors.[74]

Hospitals in Spain are concentrated in urban and metropolitan areas, particularly in and around large cities such as **Madrid, Barcelona, Valencia, Seville**, and **Bilbao**. These regions not only house the highest population densities but also contain the country's leading medical universities, research institutions, and healthcare infrastructure. Rural

---

72 https://spainhealthcaretourism.com/en/health-tourism-in-spain/
    frequently-asked-questions/

73 https://www.statista.com/statistics/444941/
    number-of-hospitals-in-spain-by-ownership-type/

74 https://ec.europa.eu/eurostat/statistics-explained/index.
    php?title=Healthcare_personnel_statistics#Healthcare_employment

areas are typically served by smaller regional hospitals or health centers, with patients referred to larger hospitals for complex procedures.

Spain is home to some internationally recognized hospitals. Among the best **public hospitals**, the **Hospital Universitario La Paz** in Madrid is frequently ranked at the top for its quality of care, innovation, and medical specialties.

Other top public hospitals include **Hospital Clínic de Barcelona**, **Hospital General Universitario Gregorio Marañón** in Madrid, and **Hospital Universitari Vall d'Hebron** in Barcelona. In the private sector, **Clinica Universidad de Navarra** (Madrid and Pamplona) and **Hospital Quirónsalud** (with branches in Madrid, Barcelona, and Marbella) are considered leading facilities, especially for international patients seeking premium care.

Many hospitals across Spain, especially private ones, are well-equipped to serve international visitors. These facilities often have **dedicated international patient departments**, English-speaking staff, and services tailored to medical tourists or expats. Hospitals like **Quirónsalud Barcelona, Hospital Ruber Internacional** in Madrid, and **Vithas Xanit International Hospital in Benalmádena** (near Málaga) are examples of hospitals that cater specifically to foreigners and offer multilingual support.

While there are **no official American-branded hospitals** in Spain (such as those affiliated with U.S. healthcare networks), some private hospitals and clinics offer services comparable to U.S. standards and employ American-trained or English-speaking doctors. American embassies and consulates in Spain maintain lists of recommended English-speaking medical providers for U.S. citizens, which can serve as a valuable resource in emergencies.

Insurance Guidance

Foreign insurance plans are accepted in Spain, **but only at certain facilities**, primarily in the **private healthcare sector**. Public hospitals generally **do not bill foreign insurance directly**, unless you are an EU/EEA citizen using a **European Health Insurance Card** (**EHIC**), which grants access to public healthcare under the same terms as Spanish residents. Travelers from outside the EU—like those from the U.S., Canada, or Australia—must either **pay upfront** or show proof of **private travel insurance** that covers international care. It's important to check with your insurance provider before traveling to confirm coverage and get a list of partnered hospitals or clinics in Spain.

The **average cost** for medical services in Spain is relatively affordable compared to many other Western countries. A **non-emergency doctor's visit** at a private clinic can cost between **€50 and €100** (US$54 to $107). A visit to the **emergency room** may range from **€100 to €200** (US$107 to 214), depending on the severity of the issue and the tests required. Hospitalization, surgeries, or advanced diagnostics can increase costs significantly, but prices still tend to be lower than in countries like the U.S.[75]

In most cases, travelers **pay out of pocket** at the time of treatment, especially in private clinics or if they don't have EHIC coverage. Payment is typically accepted via **credit/debit card** or **cash**. You should then request a **detailed receipt and medical report** to submit a claim to your insurance provider for reimbursement. Some high-end private hospitals may offer **direct billing** if you hold an international insurance policy with a known provider, but it's best to confirm this in advance.

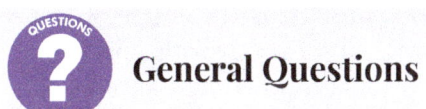

General Questions

1. *What number do I call in a medical emergency?* Dial **112**, the EU-wide emergency number, for immediate access to ambulance, police, or fire services. You can call from any phone, and English-speaking operators are available.

---

75   https://www.internationalinsurance.com/health/europe/spain.php

2. *Will I be treated if I don't have insurance?* **Yes.** Emergency medical care is provided to everyone, regardless of insurance status or nationality. However, you may be billed for treatment if you don't have a European Health Insurance Card (EHIC) or private insurance.

3. *Can I find English-speaking doctors in Spain?* **Yes.** This is especially true in major cities and tourist areas. Many private hospitals and some public ones have English-speaking staff or interpreters. For rural areas, having a translation app or phrasebook helps.

4. *Should I go to a public or private hospital?* Public hospitals offer quality emergency care, but private hospitals may have shorter wait times and more English-speaking staff. If your travel insurance covers private care, that may be your best option.

5. *Do I need to pay upfront for medical treatment?* In public hospitals, EU citizens with an EHIC usually don't pay upfront. Non-EU travelers may need to pay at the time of service and seek reimbursement from their travel insurance later, especially in private facilities.

6. *What if I need a prescription in Spain?* You'll need to visit a doctor first to get a local prescription. Most medications must be dispensed by a pharmacist, but pharmacies are common, and many are open 24/7 in any major city.

7. *Can I bring my medication to Spain?* **Yes.** However, it's best to bring your medication in the original packaging with a **prescription or doctor's note**, especially for controlled substances. Check customs rules if you're carrying large quantities.

DRIVING IN SPAIN

DRIVING IN SPAIN

Overview

Driving in Spain is generally a smooth and efficient experience, especially on major highways and well-traveled routes. The country boasts a **modern and well-maintained road network**, particularly in urban centers and along the major **autovías** (**dual carriageways**) and **autopistas** (**toll highways**). These roads are clearly marked, well-lit, and usually in excellent condition. Secondary roads and rural routes can be narrower and less maintained but are still generally safe and navigable.

Foreign drivers can legally drive in Spain with their **home country driver's license** if they are from an **EU/EEA country**. Visitors from **non-EU countries**, like the U.S., Canada, or Australia, **must carry an International Driving Permit** (**IDP**) along with their national license. Additionally, all drivers must have **valid car insurance**—either their own if driving a rental car or an international policy that covers Spain. Rental companies typically provide basic insurance (third-party liability), but travelers may want to purchase additional coverage for peace of mind.

Spain follows standard European driving rules—driving is on the **right-hand side**, seatbelts are mandatory, and using a mobile phone while driving is prohibited unless hands-free. However, a few local customs or practices may surprise foreign drivers. For example, at many roundabouts, Spanish drivers often use the **outside lane even when exiting from an inner lane**, which can be confusing. Also, flashing headlights usually means "I'm coming through," not "go ahead" as in some countries. Horn use is more regulated—generally only allowed in emergencies or to warn of danger.[76]

Spain has an extensive network of **toll roads** (*autopistas de peaje*), especially along the Mediterranean coast and in areas with heavy tourism or commercial traffic. Toll amounts vary by distance and region but generally range from **€5 to €20** (US$5.35 to $21.40) for common stretches. Payment can be made at toll booths using **cash, credit/debit cards**, or an **electronic toll tag** system called **Telepeaje** (VIA-T). VIA-T users can pass through specific lanes without stopping, which is useful for frequent travelers.[77]

Main Traffic Rules & Road Safety Tips

- **Driving Side:** Right-hand side of the road; overtake on the left.

- **Speed Limits:** (Always check signage—limits may vary)
  - 120 km/h (75 mph) on highways
  - 90 km/h (56 mph) on secondary roads
  - 30–50 km/h (18–31 mph) in towns and cities

- **Traffic Signals:** Standard European-style; red = stop, green = go, amber = prepare to stop. Flashing amber may mean yield.

- **Seat Belts:** Mandatory for all passengers, front and rear. Fines apply for non-compliance.

- **Alcohol:** Legal blood alcohol limit is 0.05 percent (0.03 percent for new drivers and commercial drivers, and 0.00 for drivers under

---

76 https://www.rac.co.uk/drive/travel/country/spain/

77 https://www.autopistas.com/en/

18). Spain has strict DUI enforcement, with random breath tests common.

- **Mobile Devices:** Use of handheld devices is prohibited. Hands-free systems are allowed, but you must not be distracted. Fines are strict.

- **Toll Roads:** Common on highways (especially along the coast and in Catalonia). Tolls range from €5 to €20 (US$5.35 to $21.40). Accepted payment methods: cash, credit/debit cards, or VIA-T (Telepeaje) tags.

- **If Stopped by Police:** Remain in the car unless told otherwise. Show passport, driver's license (and IDP if required), vehicle documents, and insurance. Spanish police are professional and may speak basic English. Fines can sometimes be paid on the spot (with a discount for prompt payment).

- **Road Safety Tips:** Watch for sudden changes in road type; rural and mountain roads can be narrow and winding. Keep an eye out for scooters and cyclists in cities. Be cautious in roundabouts— local drivers may not signal consistently.

- **Road Safety:** Spain has a low traffic fatality rate compared to other countries, thanks to strong enforcement of seat belts, speed limits, and drunk driving laws.

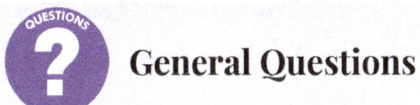 ## General Questions

1. *Can I use my driver's license from my home country to drive in Spain?* **Yes.** But only if you're from an **EU/EEA country** is your home license is valid in Spain. If you're from a **non-EU country**, you'll need to carry both your **national driver's license** and an **International Driving Permit (IDP)** to legally drive in Spain.

2. *What is the age requirement for renting a car in Spain?*
   The minimum age to rent a car is generally **21**, but some companies may require drivers to be **23 or even 25**, depending on the type of car. Most rental agencies also require the driver to have held a license for at least one year, and young driver surcharges may apply to those under 25.

 **Law of the Land Hypothetical**

HYPOTHETICAL: *Maria, a traveler from the United States, is driving a rental car along the Costa del Sol. While navigating a roundabout in Málaga, she accidentally enters the outer lane but continues all the way around to take the third exit. A local driver honks, and a traffic officer later pulls her over and issues a warning. Maria is confused— she followed what seemed like normal driving behavior. Is it illegal in Spain to stay in the outer lane of a roundabout while taking an exit that isn't the first one?*

ANSWER: *Technically, yes. In Spain, drivers are expected to use the inner lanes of a roundabout when going beyond the first or second exit and then signal and move to the outer lane before exiting. Staying in the outer lane all the way around without changing lanes can be considered incorrect use of the roundabout, especially if it causes confusion or interferes with other vehicles. While enforcement varies, it can lead to fines if deemed dangerous or if an accident occurs. It's a common point of confusion for foreign drivers, so travelers should familiarize themselves with roundabout rules and always signal clearly when changing lanes or exiting.*

NUDE BEACHES & CLOTHING-OPTIONAL RESORTS

NUDE BEACHES & CLOTHING-OPTIONAL RESORTS

Overview

Nudism is **widely accepted** in Spain and is considered a normal part of the culture, especially around the coastlines and islands. The country has a long tradition of embracing naturism, and public nudity is actually legal throughout Spain as long as it is not done in a way that disturbs public order. In practice, while you could technically be nude on any beach, most people stick to specific beaches that are well-known for being nudist-friendly. Spanish culture tends to be relaxed about bodies and beach life, especially in coastal regions and islands like Catalonia, Andalusia, and the Balearic Islands.

There are many beaches in Spain where nudism is common and completely accepted. Some of the most famous are **Playa de Ses Illetes** and **Playa Es Cavallet** in Ibiza, **Playa de los Muertos** in Almería, **Playa de Bolonia** near Tarifa, and **Playa de Maspalomas** in Gran Canaria. On these beaches, naturists and clothed visitors often mix freely without any issues. In general, naturist beaches are well-respected and clearly signposted, but even on regular beaches, you will often find people sunbathing nude without much fuss.

Spain also has a number of hotels and resorts dedicated to naturists. Some are completely nudist, while others are clothing optional. Examples include **Vera Playa Club Hotel** in Almería, which is famous for being Spain's first naturist hotel and is located right next to a full naturist urbanization where nudity is allowed even in the streets. In the Canary Islands, there are resorts like **Magnolias Natura** in Gran Canaria, which cater specifically to nudists looking for a warm, sunny getaway. Many naturist resorts in Spain offer pools, spas, beaches, and even private villas, all with a very casual and body-positive atmosphere.

Legality and Safety

Nudism in Spain is regulated more by general law and social custom rather than strict rules. **Public nudity is legal under Spanish national law** — meaning it is not a criminal offense to be nude in public spaces, including beaches. However, local municipalities do have the power to create ordinances that can restrict nudity in certain areas if they believe it is necessary to maintain public order. That said, outright bans are rare, and Spain remains **one of the more nudist-friendly countries in Europe.** Most of the regulation happens informally: nudists tend to gather in traditionally accepted spots, while more conventional beaches remain clothed by custom rather than law.

When it comes to **nudist etiquette** in Spain, it's mostly based on respect and common sense. First, always check if nudism is appropriate in the place you're visiting—either by signage, the general behavior of others, or by researching beforehand. On nudist beaches, everyone is expected to be relaxed about nudity and not to stare at others. Photography is generally frowned upon unless you have permission, because privacy is highly respected. Bringing a towel to sit on is considered basic good manners, whether you are at the beach or in a naturist resort. Public displays of affection should stay discreet, just like on any regular beach. And even though nudity is allowed, loud or disruptive behavior is still unwelcome, just as it would be in any shared public space.

General Questions

1. *Are there naturist resorts or areas where I can stay nude outside the beach?* **Yes.** There are several naturist resorts and even entire neighborhoods dedicated to nudism, such as Vera Playa in Almería, where you can walk around nude not only at the beach but also in the streets, shops, and hotel areas. There are also nudist resorts in places like Gran Canaria and Catalonia, offering everything from nudist pools and spas to fully clothing-optional villas, making it easy to enjoy a full naturist holiday.

2. *Do I have to be nude if I visit a nudist beach in Spain?* **No.** You don't have to be nude if you visit a nudist beach, but it is generally encouraged to respect the spirit of the place. Most naturist beaches are very relaxed and welcome everyone, but if you stay clothed among mostly nude visitors, it might make you stand out a bit. If you're not ready to go fully nude, simply being discreet and respectful is perfectly fine—no one will pressure you, but blending in often makes the experience more comfortable for everyone.

3. *Are there special rules for families or children at nudist beaches in Spain?* Families and children are completely welcome at naturist beaches in Spain. Nudism is seen as a natural and healthy lifestyle, not something sexualized. There are no special rules for children beyond the usual expectations of good behavior and respect for others. Many Spanish families visit nudist beaches together, and it's very normal to see all generations enjoying the beach without clothing in a relaxed, body-positive environment.

 **Law of the Land Hypothetical**

HYPOTHETICAL: *Sophie, a solo traveler, visits a well-known nudist beach in Gran Canaria. She enjoys the relaxed atmosphere and decides to take a few selfies to remember the day. While taking her photos, she accidentally captures other beachgoers in the background. A nearby couple notices and confronts her, saying that photography is not allowed.*

Is it illegal to take photos on a nudist beach in Spain if other people are accidentally included?

ANSWER: *While taking personal photos is not illegal in itself, Spanish law strongly protects personal privacy, especially in sensitive situations like nudist environments. If Sophie photographs other individuals without their consent, even unintentionally, she could be violating their right to privacy. If someone feels their privacy has been infringed, they could file a complaint, and Sophie could face legal consequences, especially if the photos are shared publicly. On nudist beaches, the general rule is to avoid taking any pictures that include others unless you have clear permission. It's best for Sophie to delete any photos that accidentally captured other people to avoid any problems.*

UNUSUAL LAWS

UNUSUAL LAWS

Overview

Unusual laws can be fascinating glimpses into a culture's values and history. While most people are aware of common legal restrictions, it's often the strange and quirky laws that capture our attention. These regulations can range from the amusing to the absurd, reflecting the unique circumstances and traditions of a place. Whether they arise from historical events, societal norms, or simply peculiar local customs, unusual laws can provide insight into the quirks of human behavior and governance.

 ## Spain's Unusual Laws and Associated Penalties

Spain has a number of unique or quirky laws that often reflect the country's history, culture, and regional diversity. Here are a few examples, along with the potential penalties for breaking them:

Ban on Swearing in Public

In some parts of Spain, particularly in places like the city of Benidorm and the Balearic Islands, there are local laws that prohibit swearing or using offensive language in public spaces. These laws are often tied to preserving public order and preventing disturbances in tourist areas.

Penalty: Breaking this law could result in a fine, which varies by region. In some places, fines can range from €50 to €500 (approximately US$54 to $540), depending on the severity of the offense.

Ban on Walking Around Barefoot in Public Places

In certain areas of Spain, walking around barefoot in public spaces—especially in restaurants, shops, or public transportation—can be considered an offense. It is more common in tourist-heavy areas or places that have strict hygiene or safety standards, such as in restaurants or cafes.

Penalty: Penalties for walking barefoot in some public spaces can range from a small fine, usually around €50 to €100 (approximately US$54 to $108) to being asked to leave the premises. It's a rare occurrence but can happen in more regulated areas.

"No Eating or Drinking in Public Parks" (Sometimes)

In cities like Madrid or Valencia, some parks and public spaces have restrictions on eating or drinking. This law is mostly aimed at keeping the spaces clean and preventing waste. It is also more common in highly regulated parks where food or drink could damage public property or wildlife.

Penalty: Fines for eating or drinking in restricted areas can range from €50 to €300 (approximately US$54 to $324). These laws are often enforced in more touristic areas where cleanliness is prioritized, or at certain times to maintain order.

"Bullfighting Law" (Animal Protection)

While bullfighting is a long-standing cultural tradition in Spain, it is also subject to certain modern animal protection laws. For example, in regions like Catalonia, bullfighting has been banned since 2010 due to animal rights concerns, while other regions still allow it but under increasingly strict regulations.

Penalty: If someone organizes or participates in a bullfight in a region where it is banned, the penalties could include fines of up to **€100,000** (approximately US$108,000) or even jail time, depending on the case's severity. In other regions, penalties may apply to those breaking animal protection laws related to the treatment of the bull.

"Owning a Dog without a License" Law

In some regions of Spain, particularly in Madrid, Catalonia, and Valencia, dog owners are required to obtain a license for their pets. This license ensures that dogs are properly vaccinated and trained. If a dog is found without proper identification or if it behaves aggressively, the owner can face fines.

Penalty: Fines for not having the proper dog license can range from **€150 to €500** (approximately US$162 to $540). If the dog is involved in an incident, such as a bite, the penalty could be much higher and might include the seizure of the animal.

 **General Questions**

1. *Is it illegal to drink alcohol on public beaches in Spain?* In certain tourist areas, like Benidorm, local authorities enforce laws prohibiting alcohol consumption on beaches to maintain order and prevent disturbances.

2. *Are there restrictions on playing loud music in public places in Spain?* **Yes**. Spain enforces noise regulations, especially in public transport and residential areas, where playing loud music or making excessive noise can lead to fines.

3. *Can I take photos inside museums or historic sites in Spain?*
Many museums and historic sites in Spain allow photography, but some places prohibit taking pictures, especially of certain artifacts or with flash. Always check the signs or ask before snapping a photo.

4. *Is it illegal to leave your car idling in Spain?* In certain cities, it's illegal to leave your car engine running when parked. This is seen as a waste of energy and contributes to air pollution, so be sure to turn off your engine when not in use.

Law of the Land True Story[78]

Spain, known for its progressive stance on personal freedoms, also has quirky laws regarding public nudity. While public nudity has been legal since 1988, it is regulated by local laws, especially when it causes a public disturbance. A notable case in 2020 involved Alejandro Colomar, who entered a police station in Valencia completely naked to file a complaint. Despite carrying clothes, he refused to dress, arguing his right to be nude. The police ordered him to dress, but his defiance led to his arrest and a €1,080 (about US$1,215) fine for "disobedience."

The Spanish Supreme Court upheld the fine, emphasizing the need to maintain public order in official spaces like police stations. The ruling underscores Spain's unique legal balance: personal freedoms, including nudity, are respected, but they cannot disrupt public order or the functioning of institutions. While nudism is accepted in designated areas, this case highlights that public spaces, especially governmental ones, have stricter decorum expectations.

---

78 https://www.channelstv.com/2024/10/11/
spanish-court-upholds-fine-for-nude-police-station-visitor

TRAVELING SAFELY

TRAVELING SAFELY

Ladies Traveling Solo

Spain is generally considered a **safe destination** for solo female travelers. According to the Global Peace Index, Spain ranks 32 out of 163 countries, indicating a relatively high level of safety and peace. Many solo female travelers report feeling secure while exploring both urban and rural areas of the country.[79]

However, as with any travel destination, it's important to exercise caution and stay informed about specific areas that may pose risks. In major cities like Barcelona and Madrid, petty crimes such as pickpocketing are common, especially in crowded tourist spots like **La Rambla, La Boqueria Market**, and near the **Prado Museum**. Travelers are advised to remain vigilant and keep personal belongings secure in these areas.

Certain neighborhoods have been highlighted for potential safety concerns. For instance, the **Sacromonte district in Granada** has been noted as an area where solo female travelers should exercise increased caution. Additionally, while **Ibiza** is renowned for its vibrant nightlife, solo travelers should be aware of the party scene's associated risks, such as the possibility of drink spiking.

---

79   https://www.theladywhotravels.com/
     is-spain-safe-for-solo-female-travellers

Recent events have also seen anti-tourism protests in regions like the **Canary Islands**, with demonstrations planned in areas such as **Tenerife**. While these protests are generally peaceful, they can lead to disruptions, and travelers are advised to stay updated on local news and avoid protest areas

Here are key **safety precautions** to take as a female solo traveler in Spain:

- Stay in hotels or rentals with strong reputations and reviews from other solo travelers.
- Stick to well-lit, busy streets after dark. Plan evening transportation in advance and avoid walking alone in unfamiliar neighborhoods.
- In nightlife hotspots like Ibiza, never leave your drink unattended and be cautious accepting drinks from strangers.
- While Spain is fashion-forward, modest clothing in certain areas can help avoid unwanted attention—especially in smaller towns.
- Share your itinerary with someone you trust and check in regularly.

Traveling as a Family

Traveling with children in Spain is generally safe and comfortable, but there are some precautions to keep in mind. Spain has a strong health-care system, and both public hospitals and private clinics are well-equipped to handle pediatric needs. It's important to carry your child's health insurance documents and consider travel insurance that includes children's care.

If your child takes prescription medication, bring enough for the trip along with a doctor's note, and be aware that most pharmacies can provide common medications. Tap water is safe to drink, and many restaurants offer kid-friendly dishes, though it helps to look for a *"menú infantil."*

In hot months, protect children from sun exposure by applying sun-screen regularly, dressing them in light clothing, and encouraging frequent hydration. Always keep your child close in busy areas and consider ID bracelets with your contact information in case of separation. Car rental companies typically offer car seats if reserved in advance, and while most cities are stroller-friendly, cobblestone streets can be challenging. For any emergency, dialing **112** will connect you to English-speaking responders. Keeping local hospital and pharmacy information handy adds an extra layer of security during your family trip.

Advice for All Travelers

When traveling in Spain, there are a few general things to be cautious about to ensure a safe and enjoyable experience. Petty theft, especially pickpocketing, is the most common issue, particularly in tourist-heavy areas like Barcelona, Madrid, and major transport hubs, so always keep your belongings secure and avoid displaying valuables openly. Be cautious around people offering unsolicited help or distractions, as these are often tactics used by thieves.

Use only official taxis or registered ride-sharing apps and avoid unmarked vehicles. While Spain is modern and generally tolerant, be respectful of local customs, especially in religious or rural areas. Always keep a copy of your passport in a separate location from the original and be mindful of alcohol consumption, as excessive drinking in public can attract negative attention or fines. Lastly, stay updated on local news or demonstrations, which are typically peaceful but can cause disruptions. Being aware and prepared will help you travel confidently and safely.

 # Do's and Don'ts While in Spain

- **Do** greet people with a handshake or cheek kisses in informal settings—it's part of the culture.

- **Don't** assume everyone speaks English; learning a few basic Spanish phrases goes a long way.

- **Do** try local dishes like paella, tortilla española, and churros—Spanish cuisine is a highlight.

- **Don't expect dinner early; Spaniards typically eat around 9:00 or 10:00PM.**

- **Do** respect siesta hours in smaller towns—some shops may close mid-afternoon.

- **Don't** speak loudly in public places; Spaniards value conversation but generally dislike shouting.

- **Do** dress modestly when visiting churches or religious sites.

- **Don't** wear swimwear away from the beach or pool; it's considered disrespectful in public areas.

- **Do** use public transportation—it's affordable, safe, and efficient.

- **Don't** assume jaywalking is okay; follow pedestrian signals to avoid fines.

CHAPTER 22
TOURIST TAXATION

TOURIST TAXATION

Overview

Tourism plays a vital role in Spain's broader economic framework, contributing around 12 percent to the national GDP and supporting millions of jobs across sectors like hospitality, transportation, and retail.[80] Spain consistently ranks among the world's most visited countries, welcoming tens of millions of tourists each year. Given this enormous economic impact, the government views tourism not just as a cultural exchange but as a major financial pillar that helps fuel national growth.

Tourists are required to pay specific taxes when visiting Spain primarily to offset the additional burden placed on public services and infrastructure. Popular destinations experience higher demands on everything from public transport and sanitation to health services and environmental conservation efforts. Tourist taxes serve as a way to ensure that visitors contribute fairly to the upkeep of the places they enjoy, rather than shifting the entire financial burden onto local residents.

The revenue collected from tourist taxes directly supports public services and infrastructure improvements. Funds are typically reinvested into maintaining historical sites, preserving beaches, improving transport networks, enhancing public safety, and protecting natural parks. For example, in heavily visited regions like Catalonia and the Balearic

---

80 https://chekin.com/en/blog/complete-guide-tourist-tax-in-spain/

Islands, tourist taxes are crucial for sustainable tourism development, helping local governments manage the environmental and social impacts of mass tourism while maintaining a high-quality experience for both visitors and residents.

Tourist Taxes in Spain

The most common tourist tax in Spain is the **tourist accommodation tax**, charged per person, per night at accommodations such as hotels, hostels, rental apartments, and campsites. The amount varies depending on the type of accommodation, its star rating, the time of year, and the specific region, with places like Barcelona and the Balearic Islands being especially notable for applying this tax. Accommodation taxes are usually added to your hotel bill and paid upon check-out.

In addition to the accommodation tax, there are other types of tourist-related taxes. One example is **environmental or sustainability taxes**. In regions like the Balearic Islands, an Eco-tax (known as the **Ecotasa**) is charged to tourists specifically to fund environmental conservation, preserve cultural heritage, and promote sustainable tourism practices. This tax works similarly to the tourist stay tax but is earmarked for ecological and community projects.

Another growing area is the **cruise ship passenger tax**. In major port cities such as Barcelona and Palma de Mallorca, passengers arriving via cruise ships are subject to special fees. These taxes help manage the environmental and infrastructural impact caused by the influx of visitors who typically spend only a few hours ashore but significantly strain local resources. Cruise passenger taxes are either included in the cruise fare or collected when disembarking at the port.

Certain regions are also introducing vehicle or transport-related charges. For example, Barcelona has implemented a **low-emission zone charge**, which applies to older, more polluting vehicles entering the city. In island regions, some local governments impose additional fees on rental cars during peak tourist seasons to reduce congestion and pollution.

Vehicle rental taxes are built into the rental agreement or applied at the time of pickup.

Beach access or nature park fees also exist in select locations. Some protected beaches and parks, particularly in the Balearic Islands, charge visitors a small fee to help fund maintenance, conservation efforts, and security services aimed at preserving fragile natural ecosystems. Beach or park access fees are generally paid directly at the site entrance.

Lastly, although Spain does not yet have a national air travel tax specifically targeting tourists, there have been discussions both nationally and across the European Union about introducing **green air travel taxes** in the future. These would likely focus on short-haul flights to encourage more sustainable transportation choices.

Spain has **VAT**, known locally as **IVA** (*Impuesto sobre el Valor Añadido*). IVA applies to most goods and services throughout the country, including hotels, restaurants, transportation, car rentals, and many types of shopping. The standard IVA rate in Spain is **21 percent**. However, there is a reduced rate of 10 percent that applies to certain services and products such as hotel accommodations, restaurant meals, and some transport and cultural activities. There is also a super-reduced rate of 4 percent, which is reserved for essential items like basic food products, newspapers, and books.

It's important to note that IVA is not a tourist tax as such. However, it's essential to be aware of it, as it is included in the price of most goods and services you purchase during your stay in Spain. For tourists who are residents outside the European Union, there is an opportunity to claim IVA refunds on eligible purchases. When shopping at participating stores, visitors can claim a tax refund if their purchases exceed a minimum amount and the goods are exported from the EU within 90 days. The refund process typically involves filling out a special tax-free form at the store, getting it stamped by customs upon departure, and then submitting it for a refund through a tax refund company or at a designated counter at the airport.

 **Law of the Land Hypothetical**

HYPOTHETICAL: *Anna, a tourist from the United States, visits Seville for a few days. She stays at a hotel, dines at local restaurants, and buys a couple of souvenirs. When she checks out of her hotel, she notices a charge labeled "tourist accommodation tax" on her bill, and the restaurant bills include VAT. Can Anna reclaim any of the taxes she paid during her stay in Seville?*

ANSWER: *Anna cannot reclaim the tourist accommodation tax, as this is a local tax charged by the city to help support public services and infrastructure. It is non-refundable. As for the VAT on her hotel stay and restaurant meals, she also cannot reclaim this tax. VAT on these services is not refundable to tourists in Spain. However, Anna may be able to reclaim the VAT she paid on her souvenirs, provided the total amount of her purchases exceeds the required minimum (around €90 or US$98). To do so, she would need to request a tax-free form at the store and get it stamped by customs when leaving Spain. Afterward, she can submit the form at the airport to receive her VAT refund.*

LONG-TERM STAYS

LONG-TERM STAYS

Overview

Many people choose to live in Spain long-term for its exceptional quality of life, affordable living costs, beautiful climate, and robust healthcare system. Spain offers a diverse range of regions, from bustling cities to tranquil countryside, making it suitable for a wide variety of lifestyles. The country is known for its welcoming culture, rich history, and vibrant lifestyle, offering an attractive combination of modern amenities and a relaxed pace of living. For retirees, the affordable cost of healthcare, combined with a pension or savings, makes Spain an appealing destination. Additionally, Spain's proximity to the rest of Europe allows for easy travel to neighboring countries, making it ideal for those who want a home base with the freedom to explore the continent.

Regions such as **Barcelona, Madrid**, and **Valencia** are popular among long-term residents due to their dynamic urban environments, cultural offerings, and high-quality services. These cities boast modern infrastructure, excellent public transport systems, and a wide array of shopping, dining, and entertainment options. For those seeking a more laid-back lifestyle, coastal areas like **Malaga** and **Alicante** or traditional cities like **Seville** offer a slower pace of life while still providing access to essential amenities. Whether you're drawn to the Mediterranean coast, the lively energy of larger cities, or the peace of rural Spain, there's something for everyone.

Living Costs in Spain

Cost of living in Spain is **notably lower** than in countries like the United States or Northern Europe. **Rent** in cities such as Valencia or Seville can be affordable, with one-bedroom apartments in city centers typically ranging from **€600 to €1,200 per month** (approximately US$650 to $1,300). Utility costs are relatively low, and public transport is inexpensive, with monthly metro passes in major cities costing between €40 and €55 (approximately US$45 to $60). Dining out in Spain is also quite affordable, with tapas and meals in local restaurants often costing less than in other Western European countries. While groceries are generally cheaper, imported goods can sometimes be pricier, but overall, living costs remain manageable for expats looking to live comfortably on a budget.

Housing Options for Long-Term Stays

Housing in Spain is diverse, ranging from modern apartments in the heart of cities to traditional houses in rural areas. The housing market is generally more affordable than in many Western European countries, with prices varying depending on location. In urban areas like Madrid and Barcelona, rental prices are higher compared to more rural areas, where one can find a spacious house or apartment for less. For example, in Madrid, the **average monthly rent for a one-bedroom apartment** in the city center could cost between **€1,200 and €1,800** (approximately US$1,300 to $2,000). In less expensive regions, rental prices can drop significantly, with one-bedroom apartments available for as low as **€400** (around US$430). Many expats initially prefer to rent before deciding to purchase property, especially in places like Seville or Malaga, where the property market is more accessible.

Healthcare Options Available for Long-Term Residents

Spain offers an **outstanding healthcare system**, which is available to all residents through the public system. Long-term residents who pay into the social security system are entitled to public healthcare, which is known for its high standards and affordability. Many expats choose to purchase private health insurance to avoid wait times and to access private clinics and specialists. Healthcare costs, even privately, are **generally lower** than those in the U.S. or Northern Europe, making it an appealing option for those looking to manage their healthcare costs while still enjoying excellent services.

Transportation Options

Transportation in Spain is excellent, especially in urban areas. Public transport systems, including metro, buses, and trams, are **affordable and efficient**, making it easy to get around in cities like Madrid, Barcelona, and Valencia. For those living in rural areas or coastal regions, owning a car may be more practical, although public transport is still available, especially in tourist-heavy areas.

Spain's high-speed rail system is also world-renowned, providing fast and convenient travel between major cities. A one-way ticket for local public transportation typically costs between €1.50 and €2 (approximately US$1.60 to $2.20), and the high-speed AVE trains between major cities like Madrid and Barcelona cost between €40 and €100 (approximately US$45 to $110), depending on the time of booking and class.

Language Considerations

Spanish is the official language, and while **English is commonly spoken** in tourist areas and by younger generations, learning **Spanish is essential for long-term residents**. Fluency in the language will not only help with daily activities but also facilitate integration into Spanish society. Many expats opt for language classes, and with numerous resources available, learning Spanish is quite accessible. Private Spanish language schools typically cost around €100 to €300 per month (approximately US$110 to $330), depending on the location and the intensity of the course. Although it's possible to get by with English, speaking Spanish will enhance your overall experience and allow you to feel more connected to the community.

Long-Term Visas

Spain offers several visa options for individuals who wish to live in the country for an extended period. These visas cater to different needs, including retirees, employees, entrepreneurs, and digital nomads. Here are the main types of long-term visas available for those looking to stay in Spain:

Golden Visa

The Golden Visa is a residency-by-investment program aimed at attracting non-EU citizens to invest in Spain. To qualify for a Golden Visa, applicants must invest in real estate, business, or government bonds, with a minimum investment threshold of €500,000 (approximately US$540,000). The visa grants residency rights for the applicant and their family, with the ability to renew after five years. This visa also offers the potential for citizenship after ten years of continuous residence.

Non-Lucrative Visa

The Non-Lucrative Visa is popular among retirees and individuals who wish to live in Spain without working. To qualify for this visa, applicants must show that they have sufficient financial means to support themselves and their dependents without needing to work. The minimum financial requirement varies, but applicants need to demonstrate an income or savings equivalent to at least €27,000 (approximately US$29,000) annually. This visa is typically issued for one year but can be renewed.

Work Visa (Highly Skilled Worker Visa)

For those looking to work in Spain, the Highly Skilled Worker Visa is designed for professionals who have a job offer in Spain with a Spanish employer. The applicant must meet certain qualifications and have a contract in a specialized role. This visa allows you to live and work in Spain for an initial period of one year, which can be renewed.

Entrepreneur Visa

The Entrepreneur Visa is designed for individuals who want to start a business or invest in a Spanish company. Applicants must present a viable business plan that meets the requirements of Spain's business regulations and demonstrates the potential to generate jobs or economic benefits for the country. This visa is issued for one year but can be extended if the business proves successful.

Student Visa

For students planning to study in Spain for more than 90 days, the Student Visa allows individuals to stay for the duration of their studies. Students are permitted to work part-time while studying. To qualify, applicants need to show proof of enrollment in a recognized institution and evidence of financial means to support themselves during their stay.

Digital Nomad Visa

Introduced in 2023, the Digital Nomad Visa allows remote workers and freelancers to live in Spain while working for foreign employers or clients. Applicants need to prove that they earn a minimum of €2,000 (approximately US$2,200) per month and that their work is remote and not tied to a local Spanish employer. This visa allows applicants to live in Spain for up to one year with the option to extend.

Family Reunification Visa

For those who are already residents in Spain, a Family Reunification Visa allows family members (spouse, children, parents) to join the applicant. This visa is issued to individuals who hold a valid residency permit in Spain, and they must prove their ability to financially support their family members.

Self-Employment Visa

This visa is for individuals who wish to work as freelancers or open a business in Spain. The applicant must show they have sufficient resources and a clear business plan to work legally in the country. It is ideal for independent contractors, business owners, and consultants.

Each visa type has specific requirements and documentation needed, so it's crucial to check the latest information with Spanish consulates or immigration lawyers before applying.

 **Visa Application Requirements**

To apply for a long-term visa in Spain, there are specific requirements that depend on the type of visa you're applying for. Generally, you will need to provide a **valid passport** that is at least three months beyond your intended stay in Spain. You will also need to fill out the **appropriate visa application form**, which can be found on the website of the Spanish consulate or embassy. Another requirement is **proof of sufficient financial means** to support yourself during your stay. This may include bank statements, proof of income, or pension details. (See above for specific amounts associated with different visa types.)

You will also need to submit **proof of health insurance** that is valid in Spain, especially for visas like the Non-Lucrative or Golden Visas. A **clean criminal background check** from your home country, no older than three to six months, is also required for most visa applications. Additionally, applicants may be asked to provide a **medical certificate** confirming they do not have any contagious diseases. Depending on the visa type, **proof of accommodation** in Spain might be needed, such as a rental agreement or an invitation letter.

There is also a **visa processing fee** that varies depending on the type of visa and your nationality, **typically ranging from €60 to €200** (approximately US$65 to $220). For some visa types, additional documentation may be required, such as investment proof for a Golden Visa or a job contract for a work visa.

The application process involves submitting your visa application to the Spanish consulate or embassy in your country of residence. **Long-term visa applications must be made before traveling to Spain, as they cannot be processed once you are in the country.** The consulate's website will provide specific instructions on how to book an appointment, as well as which documents you need to submit. It is important to apply well in advance, ideally three months to six weeks before your planned departure date, as processing times can vary. For example, the Non-Lucrative Visa typically takes around 20 working days to process, while the Golden Visa may take several months due to the required investment and legal procedures.

You can check the website of your local Spanish consulate for specific application instructions, appointment booking procedures, and other details. For the most accurate and up-to-date information, visiting the consulate's website or contacting them directly is essential.

 For additional visa information visit the Spanish Ministry of Foreign Affairs website at **https://www.exteriores.gob. es/ and SchengenVisaInfo** at **https://www.schengenvi-sainfo.com/spain-visa/**.

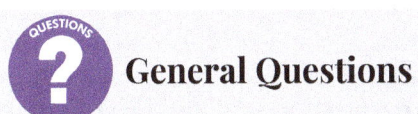 ## General Questions

1. *If I want to stay in Spain long-term and work, should I apply for a work permit before arriving in Spain?* **Yes.** If you plan to work in Spain long-term, you must apply for a work permit before arriving. Spain requires most non-EU nationals, including Americans, to obtain a work visa after securing a job offer from a Spanish employer. You cannot work in Spain on a tourist visa, so it's important to apply for the appropriate work visa at your local Spanish consulate before traveling.

2. *I am American. Can I retire to Spain?* **Yes.** As an American, you can retire to Spain by applying for a Non-Lucrative Visa, which allows you to live in Spain without working. You'll need to demonstrate sufficient financial means (around €27,000/year, or US$29,000), health insurance, and meet other visa requirements. The visa can be applied for at the Spanish consulate in the U.S. Once approved, you can live in Spain for one year and renew if you meet the criteria.

 **Law of the Land Hypothetical**

HYPOTHETICAL: *Ethan, a 35-year-old entrepreneur from Australia, wants to move to Spain and start his own business. He has a business idea for an online marketing agency and believes that Spain offers a great market for his services. Ethan has already drafted a business plan and secured funding for his venture. However, he is unsure about the specific requirements to qualify for the Entrepreneur Visa. He wants to know if his business plan needs to guarantee job creation or economic benefits for Spain, and what types of proof he will need to provide to show his business is viable.*

ANSWER: *To qualify for the Entrepreneur Visa, Ethan must submit a detailed business plan that outlines his business operations, financial projections, and how it will benefit the Spanish economy, such as through job creation or innovation. He will need to prove he has sufficient funding to establish the business, usually by showing bank statements or other financial proof. While job creation isn't mandatory, demonstrating potential for local employment will strengthen his application. Additionally, his business must comply with Spanish regulations. Ethan should ensure his qualifications and experience are evident, and consulting an immigration lawyer could help ensure a strong application.*

 **Takeaways**

- Many people choose Spain for long-term stays due to its high quality of life, affordable living costs, excellent healthcare, and diverse regions that offer both vibrant urban environments and peaceful countryside options.

- Spain offers a variety of long-term visas catering to different needs, including retirees, entrepreneurs, and digital nomads, each with specific financial and documentation requirements.

- To apply for a long-term visa, applicants must meet strict financial, health insurance, and background check requirements, and applications must be made before entering Spain.

- Visa applications should be submitted well in advance, ideally three months to six weeks before departure, as processing times can vary depending on the visa type and nationality.

CIVIL LITIGATION

CIVIL LITIGATION

Overview

Civil litigation provides a mechanism for resolving disputes, ensuring that travelers have a way to seek justice if legal issues arise while visiting another country. It helps them understand their rights and obligations under local laws, which may differ from those in their home country. The civil litigation system offers a formal process for addressing conflicts, such as contract disputes or personal injury claims, and can deter unfair practices by encouraging businesses to comply with legal standards. It also allows individuals to seek financial recourse for damages or losses and helps protect them from potential exploitation by local entities. Overall, understanding civil litigation enhances a visitor's experience and safety while traveling.

Personal Injury Claims and Compensation Law

In Spain, personal injury claims and compensation law are designed to ensure that individuals who suffer injuries due to the fault or negligence of another party are fairly compensated. A personal injury claim in Spain can be filed when an individual suffers harm or injury due to someone else's fault or negligence. Common grounds for such claims include **traffic accidents, workplace accidents, medical negligence, premises liability,** and **product liability.** The injury must be proven to have been caused by the negligent or wrongful actions of another party.

If you're injured in Spain and wish to pursue a personal injury claim, the first thing to do is **seek medical attention**, even for minor injuries. It's crucial to **report the incident to the relevant authorities**, such as the police or your employer if it occurred at work. **Documenting the incident** is essential, including taking photos of the scene, your injuries, and gathering witness contact details. **Keeping all medical records** is also vital. It's recommended to **consult with a lawyer** who specializes in personal injury law, as they can guide you through the process and help ensure you receive appropriate compensation.

In Spain, compensation for personal injuries is determined based on several factors. These include **medical costs**, which cover past and future medical expenses such as hospital bills, rehabilitation costs, and medication. **Loss of earnings** is another key factor, compensating for missed work or reduced earning capacity. **Damages for pain and suffering** are also considered, with amounts determined based on the severity of the injury and its long-term impact on your life. If the injury results in **permanent disability**, compensation will reflect the degree of impairment and its effect on your quality of life. Other damages, such as **emotional distress or loss of enjoyment of life**, may also be taken into account.

Insurance plays a significant role in personal injury claims in Spain. Many individuals and businesses have insurance that covers the costs of personal injury claims. Car insurance typically covers traffic accidents, while liability insurance covers injuries that occur on someone else's property. Employers are required to have insurance to cover workplace accidents, and health insurance can help with medical expenses. In some cases, if the responsible party has insufficient or no insurance, it may complicate the claim, but the Spanish legal system provides avenues for recourse.

Legal fees in personal injury claims can vary depending on the complexity of the case and the lawyer's fees. It's common for lawyers to work on a **"no win, no fee" basis**, meaning they only charge if they win the case. The lawyer typically receives a percentage of the awarded compensation, usually **between 10 percent and 25 percent**. Some lawyers may charge hourly rates, which can range from €100 to €300 (US$109 to $327) per hour. Additionally, court fees may be involved, which depend on the value of the claim, and expert opinions, such as medical evaluations, may add to the cost.

The duration of a personal injury claim in Spain depends on the case's complexity, the evidence available, and the parties involved. Simple cases with clear liability may be resolved more quickly, while complex cases, such as those with severe injuries or disputed liability, can take longer. Personal injury claims can typically take anywhere from a few months to several years.

How to File a Civil Claim

Filing a civil claim in Spain requires meeting specific procedural conditions. To start, a claimant must submit a **writ of claim** (*demanda*), which clearly states the facts of the case, the legal arguments, identifies all involved parties, specifies the remedy being sought, and includes all supporting evidence. If the claimant is represented by a court procedural representative (*procurador*), a **notarial power of attorney** (*poder notarial*) must also be provided. Depending on the type of case, different timelines apply: for example, in ordinary proceedings, the defendant has **20 days to respond** after being served, while in verbal proceedings—typically for claims under €6,000 (about US$6,836)—the response time is only **10 days.**[81]

Spain's legal system allows for several types of civil claims. **Ordinary proceedings** (*juicio ordinario*) are used for more complex cases or claims exceeding €6,000 (about US$6,836), while **verbal proceedings** (*juicio verbal*) handle simpler cases or those involving smaller amounts. There is also the **order for payment procedure** (*proceso monitorio*), specifically designed for uncontested monetary debts backed by documentary evidence, and the **exchange proceedings** (*juicio cambiario*), used for disputes over unpaid checks, bills of exchange, or promissory notes.

---

81 https://iclg.com/practice-areas/
    litigation-and-dispute-resolution-laws-and-regulations

Several documents are necessary when filing a claim. These include the **writ of claim**, **relevant supporting documents** such as contracts, invoices, or correspondence, **proof of payment** of any applicable court fees, **identification documents**, and if required, **a notarized power of attorney for representation**. For claims under €2,000 (about US$2,278), the procedure can be simpler: standardized forms are available and legal representation is not mandatory.[82]

Civil claims must be lodged with the court that has **territorial jurisdiction** over the case. This is typically determined by the defendant's residence, the location where contractual obligations were supposed to be performed, or where the event giving rise to the dispute occurred. Legal professionals are required to use **LexNET, Spain's electronic filing system**, while individuals without legal representation can submit documents either electronically or physically at the court's registry.[83]

Service of Documents

The service of documents in Spain is governed by the **Spanish Civil Procedure Law** (*Ley de Enjuiciamiento Civil*), particularly **Articles 149 to 162**, and, in cross-border cases, by the **Hague Service Convention**. Documents may be served through **personal delivery**, **electronic methods** (particularly via LexNET, a government-run platform for legal professionals), **registered mail**, or by **publication in official bulletins** when the recipient's location is unknown or other methods have failed.

Responsibility for serving documents typically falls on the **court clerk** (*Letrado de la Administración de Justicia*), although **judicial agents** (*agentes judiciales*), **process servers**, or **official postal services** (e.g., Correos) may assist depending on the method. For registered mail,

---

82 https://e-justice.europa.eu/topics/taking-legal-action/where-and-how/how-bring-case-court/

83 https://www.twobirds.com/-/media/disputes-plus/files/pdfs/various-qas---april-2020/service-of-claim-documents-within-the-jurisdiction-and-abroad-qanda-spain.pdf

Correos' services often cost around €5 to €10 (US$5.35 to $10.70), depending on the size and urgency.

The process starts with a court issuing the documents, followed by an attempt to serve them through personal delivery or electronic transmission. If these fail, service by registered mail or publication is used, and the results are returned to the court. Each step must comply with procedural deadlines to ensure legal validity. **Proof of service** is documented by a service certificate or acknowledgment of receipt signed by the recipient, by electronic confirmation when using LexNET, through a court-issued diligence (*diligencia*) detailing the date and method, or by a return receipt (*acuse de recibo*) from postal services.

Statute of Limitations

The statute of limitations for civil suits in Spain is primarily governed by the Spanish Civil Code. The **five-year limitation period** is the most common for civil suits based on **contractual obligations**. This includes claims such as unpaid loans, breach of contract, or failure to deliver services or goods, and is regulated by Article 1964 of the Spanish Civil Code. This limitation period begins when the obligation becomes enforceable. Before 2015, this period was fifteen years, so older contracts may still fall under the transitional rule if not expired before the reform took effect.

The **one-year limitation period** applies widely to **non-contractual liability**, commonly referred to as tort claims. This includes **personal injury**, **defamation**, or **property damage** caused by third parties, and it runs from the date the injured party becomes aware of the harm and who caused it. This is found in Article 1968.2 of the Civil Code and is one of the most common causes for legal disputes, especially in traffic accidents and medical negligence cases.

The **three-year limitation period** is often used for **professional services claims**, such as those involving lawyers, doctors, architects, and others who charge periodic or recurring fees. It also applies to rent payments, as laid out in Article 1967. This timeframe begins from when the services were provided, or the payments became due.

Real property-related civil suits, like those involving adverse possession or recovery of ownership rights, may be subject to much longer periods, such as **thirty years**, but these are far less common in day-to-day civil litigation.

Several factors can affect the duration of the statute of limitations. One such factor is **interruption**, which can occur if a formal demand is made or judicial proceedings are initiated, thereby resetting the limitation period. **Suspension** is another possibility in cases of force majeure or legal incapacity, during which the time limit is effectively paused. If a civil suit is filed after the applicable statute of limitations has expired and the defendant raises this as a defense, the court will typically dismiss the case on the grounds that it is **time-barred** (*prescripción*). While the legal enforceability of the claim is extinguished, the underlying obligation may still be acknowledged in a moral or informal sense.

There are a **few exceptions** that **may extend or delay the statute of limitations**. If the claimant is a **minor** or **legally incapacitated**, the limitation period does not begin until legal capacity is restored. Additionally, if parties are engaged in negotiations and this is mutually recognized, the limitation clock may be delayed.

 **Getting Married in Spain**

Getting married in Spain involves complying with a set of legal requirements that apply to both Spanish citizens and foreign nationals, although the process can differ slightly depending on the type of ceremony and the nationality of the couple. Legally, individuals must be **at least 18 years old** to marry without parental consent, as stipulated in Article 46 of the Spanish Civil Code.

To apply for a marriage license, the couple must present a set of documents to the local **Civil Registry** (*Registro Civil*) or to the relevant authority of a religious institution. These typically include a **valid passport or national ID, birth certificate** (with an official Spanish translation and apostille if issued abroad), **certificate of no**

impediment or single status certificate (*certificado de estado civil*), and, for foreign nationals, a **certificate of residence** (*certificado de empadronamiento*) covering the last two years. Divorced or widowed individuals must also provide the **divorce decree** or **death certificate** of the former spouse. Some municipalities may request additional documentation, so couples are advised to check with the specific registry where they plan to marry.

The process for obtaining a marriage license starts with submitting all required documents to the Civil Registry. The registry then conducts a brief administrative investigation to confirm there are no legal impediments to the marriage. Once approved, the couple receives authorization to proceed with the ceremony. The process from application to approval typically takes between **30 and 75 days**, although this can vary depending on the city and whether all documents are submitted correctly.

Foreign nationals are not required to be residents to marry in Spain, but in practice, at least one party is often asked to provide **proof of residence** (temporary or otherwise) in the local municipality. Some regions enforce this more strictly than others, so again, couples should verify local requirements in advance.

There are two main types of legally recognized marriage ceremonies in Spain: civil and religious. A **civil ceremony** is conducted by a judge, mayor, or municipal official and must take place **at the Civil Registry, town hall**, or **another authorized venue**. The couple signs the official marriage certificate during the ceremony, which is then registered with the Civil Registry. A **religious ceremony**, such as a Catholic wedding, is recognized by the state if performed by an **authorized religious official** and **later registered with the Civil Registry**. Religious marriages of other faiths (e.g., Jewish, Islamic, or Protestant) may also be recognized if the religious institution has an agreement with the Spanish state.

Fees for getting married in Spain are generally low. Civil ceremonies at the town hall or Civil Registry are often free of charge, although some cities may charge a small administrative fee ranging from €50 to €150 (US$53.50 to $160.50), depending on the venue or services provided. Religious ceremonies may involve separate fees charged by the religious institution.

Once the marriage has taken place, it must be officially registered with the Spanish Civil Registry. Registration is automatic for civil ceremonies conducted at the registry, but religious marriages require submission of the marriage certificate to the registry office to be legally recognized by the state. After registration, couples receive an official Spanish marriage certificate (*certificado de matrimonio*).

International recognition of the marriage depends on the laws of the other country. **Marriages legally performed and registered in Spain are generally recognized abroad, especially in countries that are party to the Hague Convention.** However, couples should check with their home country's consulate or embassy to ensure proper recognition. In some cases, a multilingual or Apostilled marriage certificate may be needed for use outside Spain.

 **Law of the Land Hypothetical**

HYPOTHETICAL: *Nina, a Canadian tourist visiting Seville, booked a guided horseback tour through a local adventure company. During the excursion, her horse unexpectedly bolted after being startled by loud machinery at a nearby construction site. Nina fell and suffered a fractured wrist and multiple bruises, requiring hospital treatment and forcing her to cancel the rest of her trip. She later learned that the horse she rode had a history of nervous behavior that the tour company failed to disclose. Can Nina file a personal injury claim against the tour company in Spain, and what are her chances of success as a foreign tourist?*

ANSWER: **Yes.** *Nina can file a claim in Spain even as a non-resident. Since the injury happened in Spain, local courts have jurisdiction. Under Article 1968 of the Spanish Civil Code, she has one year to file from the date she became aware of the injury and the company's potential fault. If she can prove the company knew about the horse's behavior and failed to warn her, liability for negligence is likely.*

She'll need medical records, witness statements, and any promotional material from the company. Compensation could cover medical expenses, lost enjoyment of her trip, and pain and suffering. If the claim exceeds €6,000 (around US$6,540), it will go through ordinary proceedings. Even from Canada, she can appoint a Spanish lawyer and procurador to handle the case.

OTHER THINGS TO KNOW

CHAPTER 25

OTHER THINGS TO KNOW

Tourists and Street Hustling

Street hustling in Spain is a **prevalent issue**, especially in major tourist destinations like Barcelona, Madrid, Seville, Valencia, and coastal resorts such as Benidorm and the Costa del Sol. Hustlers often engage in behaviors like aggressive solicitation, offering unsolicited items or services, and employing distraction techniques to target tourists. Common goods and services offered include counterfeit designer items, unauthorized souvenirs, and impromptu performances or games designed to elicit donations or wagers.

Tourists should be aware of several common scams: the "**lucky rosemary**" scam, where individuals offer a sprig of rosemary and then demand payment; the "**friendship bracelet**" scam, involving unsolicited bracelet tying followed by aggressive demands for money; the "**pea and cup**" street game, a deceptive betting game; **fake police officers** requesting to inspect wallets or passports; and various **pickpocketing** tactics, especially in crowded areas like La Rambla in Barcelona or the Puerta del Sol in Madrid.

Local authorities are actively addressing street hustling through increased patrols, undercover operations, and public awareness campaigns. For instance, in areas like Costa Blanca, undercover police officers have been deployed to curb illegal street vending, with tourists facing fines up to €200 (US$218) for purchasing from unauthorized vendors. Additionally, cities like Barcelona have implemented stricter regulations on short-term rentals and increased tourist taxes to manage the influx of visitors and associated issues.

Tourists are advised to remain vigilant, avoid engaging with unsolicited vendors or performers, and report any suspicious activities to local authorities. Being informed and cautious can significantly reduce the risk of falling victim to street hustling scams.

Safety Concerns and Practical Tips

Interacting with street hustlers in Spain can pose various safety concerns for tourists. These interactions may lead to theft, scams, or even physical confrontations. Hustlers often employ distraction techniques to divert attention while accomplices engage in pickpocketing or other forms of theft. In some cases, refusal to engage can result in aggressive behavior from the hustlers.

To protect themselves, tourists should remain vigilant and cautious in crowded areas, especially in popular tourist destinations like Barcelona, Madrid, and Seville. It's advisable to keep personal belongings secure and avoid displaying valuable items openly. Politely declining unsolicited offers and maintaining a firm stance can deter persistent hustlers. Being aware of common scams can also help tourists avoid falling victim to these schemes.

Understanding local customs and behaviors can further assist tourists in navigating street interactions safely. For instance, being aware that aggressive solicitation is not a typical aspect of Spanish culture can help tourists recognize and avoid potentially harmful situations. Additionally, learning basic Spanish phrases to assertively decline offers can be beneficial.

If tourists experience harassment or scams, they can report these incidents to local authorities. The Spanish National Police (Policía Nacional) and the Civil Guard (Guardia Civil) are responsible for maintaining public order and can be contacted for assistance. Tourists can also reach out to their respective embassies or consulates for support and guidance. Furthermore, the European Anti-Fraud Office (OLAF) provides a platform for reporting fraud and scams within the European Union.

 ## In the Event of Death

If someone traveling with you dies while in Spain, it's important to act promptly and follow the appropriate legal and consular procedures. The first step is to immediately **notify local emergency services** by calling **112**. Once authorities confirm the death, the local police will inform the regional judicial authority, and a forensic doctor will issue an official death certificate. You should then **contact your country's embassy or consulate** in Spain as soon as possible. They can assist with identifying the deceased, notifying next of kin if needed, explaining local procedures, and facilitating communication with Spanish authorities and funeral service providers.

The embassy or consulate cannot cover the costs involved but can help coordinate with local funeral homes, assist in obtaining official documents such as the death certificate, and provide guidance on legal procedures and translation services. If you plan to return the deceased's remains to their home country, you'll need to **work with a licensed funeral director** in Spain, who can prepare the body for repatriation and secure the necessary permits and documentation, including an international death certificate and a mortuary passport. Repatriation typically involves embalming the body and sealing it in a hermetically closed casket, in compliance with both Spanish and international transport regulations.

Families should also be aware that **repatriation costs can range from €3,000 to €6,000** (US$3,200–$6,400), depending on the location, services selected, and airline requirements. Some travel insurance policies cover these expenses, so it's important to check for coverage. Alternatively, cremation and local burial are legal and commonly available options in

Spain and may involve less logistical complexity. It's also advised to have the death registered both locally in Spain and with the deceased's home country, which the consulate can help facilitate.

Experiencing Financial Hardship

Tourists in Spain may face financial hardship for a number of reasons, including theft of wallets or cards, unexpected medical or travel expenses, poor budgeting, or frozen bank accounts due to suspected fraud. Language barriers or lack of access to online banking may further complicate the situation. If a traveler runs out of money, they should first contact their bank to determine if emergency cash transfers or temporary card solutions are available. Major banks often work with services like Western Union or MoneyGram, which have numerous branches in cities and tourist areas across Spain. It's also advisable to contact your country's embassy or consulate. While they generally cannot provide direct financial assistance, they can help arrange money transfers from family or friends and may offer guidance on local support resources.

Spain has some support systems in place for travelers in distress. **Tourist assistance centers** (such as **SATE—Servicio de Atención al Turista Extranjero**) in cities like Madrid and Barcelona offer multilingual help for tourists who are victims of crime or facing hardship. Some religious organizations or NGOs in larger cities may also offer food, shelter, or emergency aid on a short-term basis.

To avoid financial difficulties, tourists should take time to understand the euro (€) and typical local prices. For example, a basic meal costs around €10 to €15 (US$10.70–$16.05), public transportation tickets cost about €1.50 to €2.50 (US$1.60 to $2.70), and mid-range accommodations can range from €60 to €120 (US$64 to $128) per night. Having both a physical and digital backup method of payment is highly recommended.

To manage expenses while traveling in Spain, visitors should follow a few budgeting tips:

- Set daily spending limits based on pre-calculated costs for accommodation, food, transport, and attractions
- Use budgeting apps to track real-time expenses
- Carry a mix of cash and cards but avoid holding large amounts
- Take advantage of free or low-cost attractions such as museums with free entry days or walking tours
- Avoid withdrawing small amounts frequently from ATMs to minimize fees

QUICK REFERENCE GUIDE

IN THIS CHAPTER

- Quick Chapter References to Important Topics

QUICK REFERENCE GUIDE

Crime in Spain

Are there particular areas I should avoid as a tourist?

Yes. While Spain is generally safe for tourists, certain areas in major cities warrant extra caution. In Barcelona, neighborhoods like Raval can feel less secure at night, and the Gothic Quarter and El Born are common spots for pickpockets, especially around Las Ramblas and metro stations. Scams involving fake petitions, staged spills, or people posing as police also occur. In Madrid, Lavapiés and Puente de Vallecas may feel sketchy after dark, and theft is common around Puerta del Sol, Gran Vía, and Atocha station. Stick to licensed taxis or apps like Uber to avoid scams.

Cities like Seville and Valencia are generally safe, but petty theft can happen in crowded areas or during festivals. On the coast—in places like Ibiza or Magaluf—be careful with personal items on the beach and keep an eye on drinks in clubs. With basic precautions like keeping valuables secure and staying alert in crowds, most travelers have no issues. *For more details, see Chapter 3.*

Drug Offenses

Is the possession of marijuana legal?

No. The possession of marijuana is **not fully legal** in Spain. However, private personal use and cultivation in one's home are decriminalized. Public possession or consumption is illegal and can result in administrative fines, and selling or trafficking marijuana remains a criminal offense.

Is the possession of cocaine legal?

No. Cocaine possession is **not legal** in Spain. Private possession of small amounts for personal use is decriminalized but still illegal. Public possession can lead to fines, and trafficking or sale is a serious criminal offense punishable by prison. *For more details, see Chapter 4.*

Alcohol-Related Offenses

What is the legal drinking age?

The legal drinking age is 18, which means you must be at least **18 years old** to legally purchase and consume alcohol in public.

What is the legal blood alcohol limit to drive?

The legal blood alcohol limit is **0.05 percent** for most drivers and **0.00 percent** for new or commercial drivers. Penalties for exceeding these limits include fines, license suspension, and possible jail time. *For more details, see Chapter 5.*

Firearm & Ammunition Offenses

Can I possess a gun?

Yes. You can possess a gun but only under strict conditions. Firearm ownership in Spain requires obtaining a license from the Guardia Civil. Applicants must pass background checks, medical and psychological evaluations, and theoretical and practical exams. Licenses are issued for specific purposes such as hunting, sport shooting, or professional use, and self-defense licenses are rare and granted under exceptional circumstances. Carrying firearms in public is generally prohibited without special authorization.

Can I possess ammunition?

> **Yes**. You can possess ammunition but only for firearms you legally own. Ammunition purchases require presenting your firearm license and are subject to strict limits. For example, you may possess up to 200 rounds for rifles and 100 rounds for handguns at any time, with annual purchase limits of 1,000 rounds for rifles and 100 for handguns. Shotgun ammunition limits are higher, allowing up to 5,000 shells without annual purchase restrictions. Ammunition must be stored separately from firearms, and exceeding these limits can result in penalties.[84] *For more details, see Chapter 6.*

Prostitution

Is prostitution legal?

> **No**. Prostitution is **not legally regulated** in Spain, but it is **not illegal either**. Selling sex is allowed but pimping and profiting from another person's prostitution are criminal offenses. Some cities impose fines on street prostitution, and national efforts to criminalize it are ongoing but not yet law. *For more details, see Chapter 7.*

LGBTQ

Is homosexuality legal?

> **Yes**. Homosexuality is **legal** in Spain. Same-sex sexual activity has been legal since 1979, and same-sex marriage has been legal since 2005.

Are same-sex public displays of affection socially acceptable?

> **Yes**. Public displays of affection between same-sex couples are generally socially acceptable in most parts of Spain, especially in larger cities like Madrid and Barcelona, although attitudes can be more conservative in some rural areas. *For more details, see Chapter 8.*

---

84 https://mount-oregano.livejournal.com/137002.html?utm_source

Arrested in Spain

Would I be entitled to bail if I'm arrested?

Yes. In Spain you are generally entitled to bail depending on the nature and seriousness of the crime, your criminal record, and the risk of flight.

Will a lawyer be provided to me if I cannot afford one?

Yes. If you cannot afford a lawyer, the Spanish legal system will provide you with a court-appointed public defender (*abogado de oficio*) free of charge. *For more details, see Chapter 10.*

Helping a Friend or Relative Imprisoned in Spain

Can I send money to a friend or relative imprisoned in Spain?

Yes. You can send money to a friend or family member imprisoned in Spain. This is usually done through prison-approved bank transfers or postal orders, and each prison may have its own procedures.

Can I remain in the country upon release from prison or jail after my sentence is complete?

Yes. You can remain in Spain upon release from prison if you are a legal resident or citizen. However, if you are a foreign national without legal status or have committed serious crimes, you may face deportation or other immigration consequences. *For more details, see Chapter 12.*

Crime Victim Assistance

Can a victim of a crime be legally compensated?

Yes. Victims of crime in Spain can be legally compensated. Under **Law 4/2015**, victims—including those of violent crimes, sexual offenses, and terrorism—are entitled to compensation for damages such as bodily injury, property loss, and emotional harm. If the offender cannot pay, the state may provide compensation through the

Ministry of Justice. Family members of homicide victims, such as spouses, children, and parents, may also be eligible for compensation.

Can a crime victim in Spain file a civil lawsuit against the offender for damages?

Yes. A crime victim in Spain can file a civil lawsuit against the offender for damages. This can be done independently of the criminal proceedings and seek compensation for any harm caused, including physical injury, emotional distress, or property damage. The victim can claim compensation either during the criminal trial or through a separate civil court case. *For more details, see Chapter 14.*

U.S. Consulate Assistance

Are there any limitations to the consulate assistance I can receive while in Spain?

Yes. While the consulate can assist you in various matters, such as providing legal advice, contacting family, or helping with emergency travel documents, there are some limitations. The consulate **cannot** provide financial assistance, intervene in legal disputes, or offer direct legal representation. They also cannot get you out of jail or override local laws or court decisions. *For more details, see Chapter 14.*

Police

Is there an official police force?

Yes. Spain has several official police forces, with the two main ones being the **National Police** (*Policía Nacional*) and the **Civil Guard** (*Guardia Civil*). The National Police handles urban areas and matters related to national security, while the Civil Guard is responsible for rural areas, border control, and general law enforcement. Additionally, local police forces (Policía Local) operate within individual municipalities. *For more details, see Chapter 15.*

How to Get Legal Help in Spain

Is there a resource in Spain to find legal representation?

Yes. In Spain, you can find legal representation through the **Spanish Bar Association** (*Colegio de Abogados*), which has regional offices that provide information about lawyers in your area. You can also use their online directory to find legal professionals who specialize in different areas of law.

Is there free legal representation assistance?

Yes. Free legal representation is available through the **Public Defender System** (*Abogado de Oficio*), which provides legal assistance to individuals who cannot afford to hire a private lawyer. This service is available for both criminal and civil cases, depending on your financial situation.

Can a lawyer in Spain represent me in court if I don't speak Spanish?

Yes. A lawyer in Spain can represent you even if you don't speak Spanish. They can communicate with you in your own language (or via an interpreter you hire), and the courts will provide a free court-appointed interpreter during proceedings to ensure you understand everything. *For more details, see Chapter 16.*

Foreign Embassies in Spain

Are there foreign embassies in Spain?

Yes. Spain hosts over 120 foreign embassies—most are based in Madrid, with additional consulates scattered in cities like Barcelona, Valencia, and Seville.

Is there a website to locate embassies in Spain?

Yes. You can locate any embassy or consulate via the Spanish Ministry of Foreign Affairs' official directory at **https://www.exteriores.gob.es/en/EmbajadasConsulados/Paginas/index.aspx**. This site lets you search by country and city to find address, contact details, and office hours. *For more details, see Chapter 16.*

Medical Facilities & Hospitals

Is there a number I can call for ambulance and fire emergencies?

> **Yes. Dial 112** for ambulance, fire, or any other emergency anywhere in Spain. It's free, available 24/7, and operators can connect you to the appropriate service (and often speak English).

If I am injured while on vacation in Spain, are there hospitals that are recommended for tourists?

> **Yes.** Spain has several internationally accredited hospitals popular with tourists. In Madrid, for example, Hospital Universitario Fundación Jiménez Díaz, HM Sanchinarro, and Hospital Quirónsalud Madrid all have English-speaking staff and dedicated international patient services. In Barcelona, Hospital Clínic, Centro Médico Teknon, and Quirónsalud Barcelona are similarly well-regarded. These facilities combine high medical standards with experience treating foreign visitors—just be sure to carry your EHIC (if you're from the EU) or travel insurance details. *For more details, see Chapter 17.*

Driving in Spain

Which side of the road do I drive on?

> You drive on the **right side** of the road in Spain. In Spain, traffic keeps to the right, with steering wheels on the left in vehicles.

Can I use my driver's license from my home country to drive in Spain?

> **Yes.** You can use your home country driver's license to drive in Spain, provided you also carry a valid International Driving Permit (IDP) if your license isn't in Spanish, and your stay is a short-term visit (up to 90 days on a tourist visa). Under Spanish law, visitors may drive with a valid foreign license plus IDP for short visits.

How old do I need to be to rent a car?

> You must be **at least 21 years old** to rent a car in Spain; many rental companies require drivers to be 23 or older and charge a "young

driver" surcharge for those under 25. *For more details, see Chapter 18.*

Nude Beaches & Clothing-Optional Resorts

Is public nudity legal on the beaches?

Yes. Public nudity on beaches is legal in Spain. Spanish law contains no national ban on non-sexual nudity, so naturism and topless sunbathing are widely tolerated on most beaches; only a few municipalities have local ordinances restricting nudity off-beach or on streets. *For more details, see Chapter 19.*

Tourist Taxation

Is there room tax in Spain?

Yes. There is a tourist (room) tax in certain regions of Spain—known as a "green" or "ecotax"—applied per person, per night. Rates vary by region and season, typically between €0.25 and €3.50 (US$0.28 to $3.85), and are collected by the accommodation upon checkout. Regions like Catalonia and the Balearic Islands impose this tax, while others (e.g. Madrid, Andalucía) currently do not.

Is there any fee associated with leaving Spain?

No. There is no government-mandated departure or exit fee charged when you physically leave Spain. The only "exit tax" in Spanish law is a capital-gains tax on unrealized assets for high-net-worth individuals who change their tax residence—but this does not affect ordinary travelers departing by air, sea, or land. *For more details, see Chapter 22.*

Long-Term Stays

Do I need to return to my home country to apply for a work permit in Spain?

Yes. You must apply for your work permit and the corresponding national visa at the Spanish consulate in your home country (or country of legal residence) before traveling, as Spain does not permit switching from a tourist status to a work permit from within the country.

As an American, can I stay in Spain without a visa?

Yes. As an American, you may stay in Spain—and the wider Schengen Area—for **up to 90 days** within any rolling 180-day period without a visa. *For more details, see Chapter 23.*

In the Event of Death

What documents would an embassy need regarding the death of a tourist?

The embassy will require the deceased tourist's original passport (or certified copy) to confirm identity, the official death certificate issued by the local civil registry (translated and legalized), and the police or coroner's report detailing the circumstances of death. You will also need any available autopsy or medical examiner's report, a notarized affidavit or family statement proving your relationship to the deceased, and your own passport or ID as next of kin. Finally, provide flight booking or repatriation arrangements, including the forwarding address and contact details, to coordinate the return of remains. *For more details, see Chapter 25.*

EMERGENCY/IMPORTANT CONTACT NUMBERS IN SPAIN

 Please consider putting some of these numbers in your phone **prior** to traveling to Spain.

Emergency Numbers:

- **Police:** 091 (Policía Nacional) / 062 (Guardia Civil)
- **Fire:** 080 (local fire brigades; call 112 if unsure)
- **Ambulance:** 061 (regional health emergencies) / 112

Other Useful Contacts:

- **General Emergency Services:** 112 (Europe-wide single number)
- **Tourist Police (SATE):** +34 902 102 112
- **Coast Guard (Salvamento Marítimo):** 900 202 202
- **Roadside Assistance (RACE):** 900 112 222 (24 h)
- **Missing Children Hotline:** 116 000 (EU-wide)
- **Domestic Violence Helpline:** 016

Legal Assistance:

- **Spain Bar Association (Consejo General de la Abogacía Española):** +34 91 523 25 93
- **Legal Aid (Asistencia Jurídica Gratuita):** www.justiciagratuita.es or 060 (in Spain) / +34 902 887 060 (from abroad)

USEFUL SPANISH PHRASES

Greetings

HI/HELLO – Hola

GOOD MORNING – Buenos días

GOOD AFTERNOON – Buenas tardes

GOOD NIGHT – Buenas noches

GOODBYE – Adiós

Magic Words

PLEASE – Por favor

THANK YOU – Gracias

YOU'RE WELCOME – De nada

CHEERS! – ¡Salud!

EXCUSE ME – Perdón / Disculpe

Getting Around

WHERE IS THE BATHROOM? – ¿Dónde está el baño?

WHAT TIME IS IT? – ¿Qué hora es?

HOW DO I GET TO...? – ¿Cómo llego a...?

WHERE DOES THIS TRAIN/BUS GO? – ¿A dónde va este tren/autobús?

RESTAURANT – Restaurante

HOW MUCH DOES THIS COST? – ¿Cuánto cuesta esto?

TRAIN/METRO STATION – Estación de tren / metro

Communication

DO YOU SPEAK ENGLISH? – ¿Habla inglés?

I DO NOT UNDERSTAND – No entiendo

I DON'T SPEAK SPANISH – No hablo español

I DON'T KNOW – No lo sé

Emergency

HELP! – ¡Ayuda! / ¡Socorro!

CALL AN AMBULANCE! – ¡Llame una ambulancia!

I NEED A DOCTOR – Necesito un médico

POLICE – Policía

I'M LOST – Estoy perdido/a (perdido if male, perdida if female)

IT'S AN EMERGENCY – Es una emergencia

GLOSSARY

ACQUITTAL: A jury verdict that a criminal defendant is not guilty, or the finding of a judge that the evidence cannot support a conviction.

ADVERSARY PROCEEDING: A lawsuit arising from a controversy that begins with filing a complaint.

AFFIDAVIT: A written statement made under oath.

APPEAL: A request made after a trial court has decided against one party in which the losing party asks a higher court to review the decision for legal error.

ARRAIGNMENT: A proceeding in which a criminal defendant is brought to court, told of the charges, and asked to plead guilty or not guilty.

BAIL: The temporary release of a person from jail when awaiting trial, on condition that a sum of money be lodged or deposited to guarantee an appearance in court.

BARRISTER: A lawyer admitted to plead at the Bar and who may try cases in superior court.

BURDEN OF PROOF: The duty to prove disputed facts.

CAUSE OF ACTION: A legal claim in a civil action.

COMPLAINT: A written statement that begins a civil lawsuit in which the plaintiff details the claims.

CONTRACT: An agreement between two or more persons to do something or to not do something.

CONVICTION: A judgment of guilt against a person charged with a crime.

CUSTOMS DUTY: A tariff or tax imposed on goods when transported across international borders.

COURT LIAISON: A person that coordinates with attorneys to perform administrative duties, such as scheduling witnesses, sharing information with law enforcement, and overseeing the reporting of cases to foreign embassies when applicable.

DAMAGES: Money that a defendant pays to a plaintiff in a civil case if the plaintiff wins.

DEFENDANT: 1) The individual against whom a civil claim is filed; 2) The individual against whom a criminal claim is filed.

FELONY: A serious crime, punishable by more than one year in prison.

MAGISTRATE: A judicial officer of a district court, who conducts initial proceedings in criminal cases, decides criminal misdemeanor cases, conducts many pretrial civil and criminal matters on behalf of district judges, and decides civil cases with the consent of the parties.

MISDEMEANOR: An offense punishable by one year or less in jail.

PLAINTIFF: A person or business that files a formal complaint with the court.

PLEA: In a criminal case, the answer of "guilty," "not guilty," or "no contest" in response to a criminal charge.

SOLICITOR: A lawyer who advises clients, represents them in lower court, and prepares cases for barristers to try in higher courts.

SOVEREIGN IMMUNITY: A legal doctrine by which the sovereign or the state (i.e. government) cannot commit a legal wrong and thus, it is immune from criminal and civil liability and cannot be sued.

STATUTE: A written law passed by a legislative body.

STATUTE OF LIMITATIONS: A statute prescribing a period of limitation to bring certain types of legal actions. If the action is not brought within that time, the person or entity (in a criminal context) is permanently barred from suing in court.

SUBPOENA: A command, issued under court authority, for a witness to appear and to give testimony.

TESTIMONY: Evidence presented orally by witnesses.

VERDICT: The decision of a judge or jury in a case.

WARRANT: Court authorization to conduct a search or to make an arrest.

ACKNOWLEDGMENTS

This book series would never have seen the light of day without the able assistance of the following people:

Kathy Adams, my paralegal for over 22 years, who is the "Best" I've ever worked with during my entire legal career because of her amazing work ethic, organizational skills, and her ability to think outside of the box in unique and creative ways;

Ally Knez-Siddique, a professional writer, and one of my paralegals, whose eye for detail, according to her, is both a blessing and a curse;

Gino Ibanez, my former law clerk, whose exceptional research skills helped move this book series along in its early stages;

Rosa Diaz Graham, my legal assistant who helped with research and word processing at the very beginning of this project;

Shelia Martin, one of my former paralegals, worked diligently on this series of books, even after taking on another job. Her organizational skills are reflected throughout;

Mindy Scarlett, my marketing and publishing "Guru"! Her creativity and vision have no boundaries!

ABOUT THE AUTHOR

Michael L. Moore practices in Orlando, Florida, the city where he spent his formative years. He credits the trauma of having his brother murdered when he was only 10 years old, as the catalyst that drew him into the practice of law.

Moore attended Florida State University, where he was a member of the FSU debate team. Upon graduating, he was awarded a full scholarship to attend the University of Tennessee College of Law, where he was elected President of the Student Bar Association. He further honed his advocacy and public speaking skills by participating in 'moot court' competitions.

After clerking at the Tennessee Attorney General's office while in law school, Moore moved back to Orlando, Florida, to work at the State Attorney's Office as a prosecutor, and where he was fortunate enough to meet the young lady that would eventually become his wife. Moore moved on to working for private law firms, both local and national, and eventually established his own law firm in 1999. He continues to make Orlando his home base.

It was the murder of a close friend and client in Jamaica that caused Moore to realize that books on laws in other countries were few and far between, and he was inspired to create Law of the Land Publishing. Moore launched Law of the Land Publishing to provide a series of guide-books and a membership site for tourists and business travelers to stay up to date on the laws in each country they travel to, as well as having access to assistance if they run into legal issues.

"My vision is to educate people on what their legal rights are, and how they can access legal assistance, no matter where they have to travel to in the world," said Moore. "As Americans, we have a right to due process, but in some countries, you don't even have the right to access a square meal when incarcerated. My goal is to provide the information needed to stay out of trouble, as well as having access to assistance if trouble finds you."